AQA

KS3

Activate
Know • Apply • Extend

2

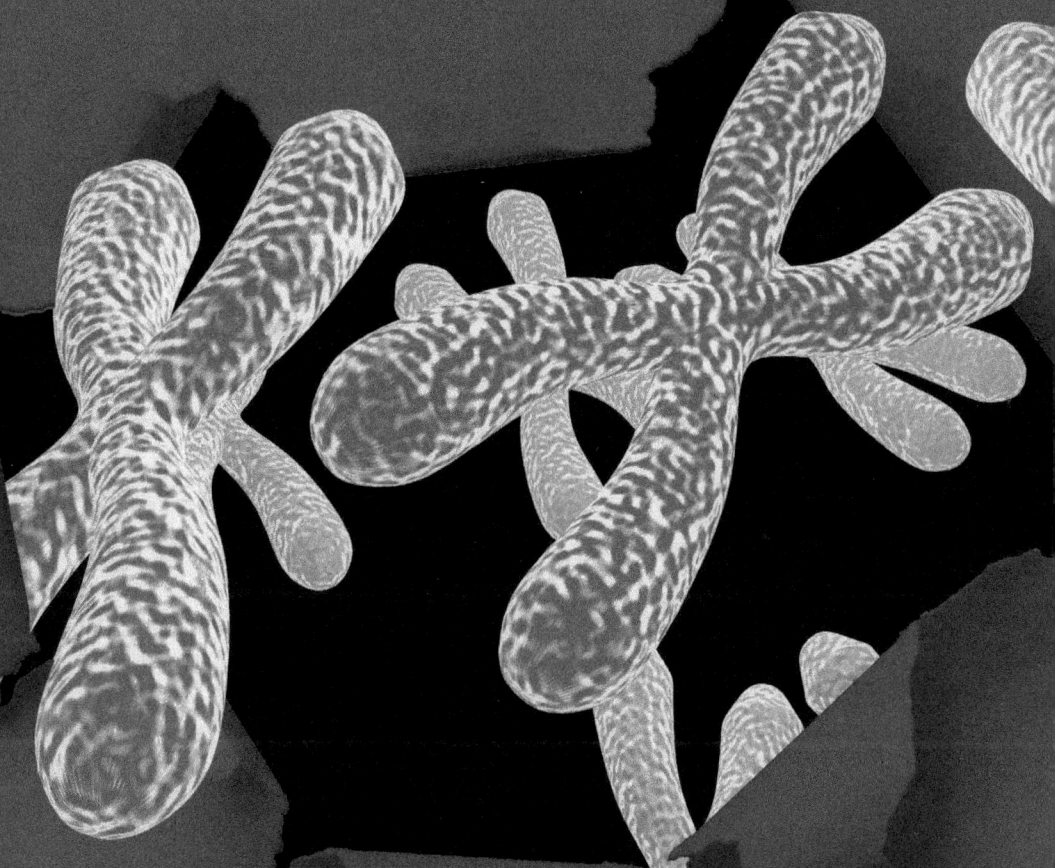

Workbook: Higher
Including Diagnostic Pinchpoint activities

Jon Clarke
Philippa Gardom Hulme
Jo Locke

Assessment Editor
Dr Andrew Chandler-Grevatt

OXFORD
UNIVERSITY PRESS

Contents

Introduction

Welcome to your *AQA Activate* 2 Workbook. This Workbook contains lots of practice questions and activities to help you to progress through the course.

Each chapter from the *AQA Activate* 2 Student Book is covered and includes a summary of all the content you need to know. Answers to all of the questions are in the back of the Workbook so you will be able to see how well you have answered them.

Practice activities – Lots of questions and activities, increasing in difficulty, give you plenty of practice and help to build your confidence.

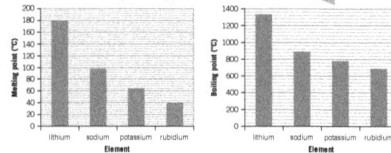

Hints – Helpful hints give you extra guidance on how to answer harder questions.

Revision questions – At the end of each of the sections you will find revision questions. These are exam-style questions to test your knowledge. They include a mix of short- and long-answer question types, as well as maths questions. Questions with two conical flasks next to them are the easiest; questions with three flasks are harder.

Checklists – Revision checklists at the end of each section cover the content in the revision questions. You can tick the boxes to show how confident you feel with each area. The Maths icon shows that you will need to use your maths skills to answer the question.

Pinchpoints

A Pinchpoint is an idea or concept in science that can be challenging to learn. It is often difficult to say *why* these ideas are challenging to learn. The Pinchpoint intervention question at the end of each chapter focuses on a challenging idea from within the chapter. By answering the Pinchpoint question you will see whether you understand the concept or whether you have gone wrong. By doing the follow-up activity you will find out why you made the mistake and how to correct it.

Pinchpoint question – The Pinchpoint question is about a difficult concept from the chapter that students often get wrong. You should answer the Pinchpoint question and one follow-up activity. The Pinchpoint is multiple choice; answer the question by choosing a letter and then do the follow-up activity with the same letter.

Big Idea 4 Pinchpoint

Pinchpoint question

Answer the question below, then do the follow-up activity with the same letter as the answer you picked.

Annabelle is analysing the motion of the ground during a recent earthquake. The diagram shows how the ground shifted while a disturbance moved in the direction of the arrow.

She is wondering whether a transverse wave is a good model for this phenomenon.

Select the best answer below.

A No, it is not a good model. In a wave, particles travel the whole length of the wave. However, no part of the ground moved that far – each part just oscillated around one place.

B No, it is not a good model. In a transverse wave, the oscillation is parallel to the direction of the wave. However, here the ground oscillated at right angles to the direction the wave moved.

C Yes, it is a good model. Waves do not transfer energy, and no energy was transferred during the earthquake.

D Yes, it is a good model. In transverse waves, energy is transferred at right angles to the direction of the oscillations.

Follow-up activities

A A transverse wave consists of a series of oscillations, which move along the wave.

  a Fill in the labels on the diagram using these keywords.

  | wavelength | energy transfer | oscillations |

  b Describe how the direction of movement of the particles in the spring relates to the direction of energy transfer.

  Hint: What direction are the oscillations in a wave? For help, see 4.4.1 Modelling waves.

B a This diagram shows a sound wave, which is a longitudinal wave.
  Describe how the motion of the air particles compares to the motion of the wave.

b This diagram shows a water wave, which is a transverse wave, moving to the right.
  Describe how the motion of the water particles compares to the motion of the wave.

Hint: What is the difference between a transverse and a longitudinal wave? For help, see 4.4.1 Modelling waves.

C a Fill in the gaps to complete the sentences about energy and work.

  Work done is defined as _____ times _____ if 1 J of work is done then _____ J of energy must have been _____ between energy stores. Changing the shape of an object requires applying a _____ and pushing it through a _____. Destroying a building means that _____ was done and _____ was required.

  b Complete the sentences about energy transfer using these keywords.

  | gamma ray | infrared | turbine | ionise | water waves |

  Electricity can be generated by _____, because they transfer energy while moving a _____. _____ radiation heats an object when it is absorbed. A _____ transfers enough energy to _____ an atom, removing an electron from it.

  Hint: Which kinds of waves can transfer energy? For help, see 4.3.1 Sound waves, water waves, and energy, and 4.3.2 Radiation and energy.

D The diagram shows two types of waves that occur during earthquakes. These can only travel along the surface of the Earth and appear after P- and S-waves.

  Suggest what happens to a structure such as a road or house when one of these waves reaches it.

⊗ **Pinchpoint review**
Now look back at the question – do you think you chose the right letter?
Turn to the Answers page to find out.

Pinchpoint follow-up – The follow-up activities will help you to better understand the difficult concept. If you got the Pinchpoint question right, the follow-up will develop your understanding further. If you got the Pinchpoint wrong, it will help you to see why you went wrong, and how to get it right next time.

EP6 More on planning how to answer a question

A Fill in the gaps to complete the sentences.

You can investigate a question scientifically if you can collect _____. This can be in the form of

observations or _____. The variable you change in an investigation is the _____

variable. The _____ variable is what you measure or observe. It is important to _____

all other variables so they don't affect the result.

You should compare the results of your investigation with others. If they are similar, the investigation is

_____.

B Sort the following questions into the type of scientific enquiry you should carry out.

1 How does temperature affect the rate of a chemical reaction?
2 How are reusable bags different from each other?
3 What is the best material for making a coat?
4 Which is the nicest flavour of fizzy drink?
5 How do leaves on a holly bush vary?
6 How does the number of coils around a magnet affect its strength?

Observational enquiry	Pattern-seeking enquiry	Not a scientific enquiry

C In all scientific investigations, it is important to control variables. Explain why.

_____

_____

D A group of students decided to investigate whether eating breakfast affected the number of press-ups they could complete at 11 a.m.

a Name the independent variable. _____

b Name the dependent variable. _____

c Give **two** examples of control variables. _____, _____

E A group of students wanted to investigate what the best material is for making a reusable bag.

a Explain why this is not a scientific question.

_____

_____

b Suggest **two** alternative scientific questions that could be investigated, which could help them to decide which is the 'best' material for making a reusable bag.

1 _____

2 _____

EP7 More on analysing and evaluating

A Fill in the gaps to complete the sentences.

To identify trends on a graph you should add a line of _____ _____. This should have

approximately the _____ number of data points above and below the line.

Any data you use in an investigation that you have not collected is called _____ data. If this data

matches your findings you can have more confidence in your _____.

B A student made four attempts at drawing a line of best fit on her graph.

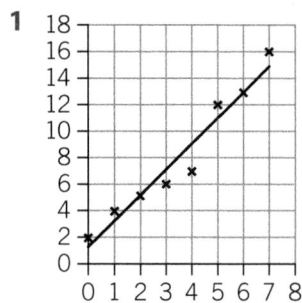

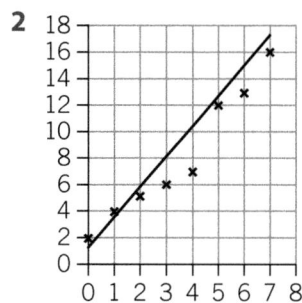

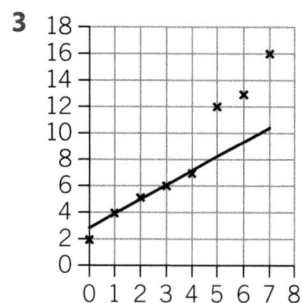

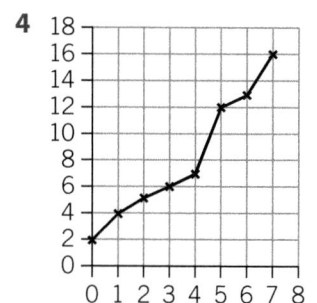

a Identify the graph with the correct line of best fit. _____

b For the other graphs, describe the mistake the student made.

Graph _____ _____

Graph _____ _____

Graph _____ _____

C Describe two things you should do if your conclusion does not agree with your prediction.

1 _____

_____

2 _____

_____

D In an investigation, if you only collect a small range of data it limits what conclusions you can make.

a Describe how changing the range and interval for the variable could provide more confidence in your conclusion.

_____

_____

_____

_____

b Give **two** reasons why it may not be possible to make these changes to an investigation.

1 _____

2 _____

EP8 Communication

A Fill in the gaps to complete the sentences.

To make communication _____, you need to consider who will _____ it; for example, young children, the general public, or other scientists. This is called the _____. You also need to consider what the writing is intended to achieve: for example, to interest people, explain an idea, or allow scientists to carry out your experiment. This is called the _____.

B Draw a line to match each sample of writing with its intended purpose.

a Today, scientists at the University of Budmouth announced that they have used a 'force field' to move matter. Like something in a science fiction film, they used beams of ultrasound to move plastic beads.	**1** Scientific journal
b Two ultrasound waves were superposed to produce a maximum upwards force of 12 millinewtons. The plastic beads were displaced up to a maximum of 10 mm horizontally and held to their position with a precision of 1 mm.	**2** Worksheet for primary school children
c Forces are pushes or pulls. You can even use invisible waves to lift something.	**3** Newspaper

C A group of students wrote the passage below recording a procedure they used.
"We measured the height of the step. The height of the step was measured using a 50 cm ruler. It was careful."
Identify two places where the writing could be improved and explain why they need improvement.

_____

_____

D Writing for scientific journals and scientific magazines is different because each is intended for a different audience. Explain **two** differences between the two types of writing.

_____

_____

_____

_____

EP9 Evidence and sources

A Fill in the gaps to complete the sentences.

Scientists use _____ to help them reach conclusions. Other scientists conduct a _____

before the work is published in a _____.

An organisation that pays for scientific research is a _____. This can lead to _____.

B In 1989, two scientists, Fleischmann and Pons, reported some new work on the topic of 'cold fusion' directly to the media. This was two weeks before it completed peer review at a scientific journal.

Explain how peer review would have made their claims more believable.

_____

_____

C Bias will occur in many situations concerning scientists' work.

Draw a line to match each situation with a possible bias it might cause.

a A scientific adviser to the government is fired after publishing an article stating that the available scientific evidence contradicts a government policy.	**1** Scientists are less likely to give impartial advice that matches best available evidence, in case they lose their job.

b Scientific journals favour publishing new research, rather than attempts to replicate other scientists' work.	**2** Scientists are more likely to discard a measurement as an anomaly if it does not fit their preferred theory.

c A scientist has previously argued that a particular theory is correct, even though repeatability of results was an issue. He has continued to research the topic and has just obtained a new measurement.	**3** Scientists are less likely to test existing work, so scientific mistakes and misunderstandings are less likely to be uncovered and corrected.

D Complete the sentences below about the effects of different sources of funding. Use the keywords in the box.

guarantee	reporting	deny	experimentation	requires	never

Funding for scientific research can be provided by a government or a university. If the source of funding is from a

university it might affect _____. A limited amount of money might _____ access to an

expensive piece of equipment as it is not sufficient to purchase it outright. However, a grant from a university that

already owns that equipment might _____ access to it.

If the source of funding is from the government, it might affect _____. Some government funding

_____ publishing in "open access" journals, where anyone can read the results without paying a fee.

However, a commercial company might want the results _____ to be published, so that they keep

an advantage over rival companies.

EP10 Critique claims and justify opinions

A Fill in the gaps to complete the sentences.

People and organisations may make a claim, which is a statement that says that something is _____.
To decide whether a claim is believable, you need to look at the scientific _____ that is offered to
support or oppose a claim. Evidence can include measurements, data, and _____. You also need to
use reasoning to help you to decide what the evidence means and to make an _____ for or against a
claim. If you give an opinion about a claim, you must use scientific _____ to justify your opinion.

B Read the news article in the box.

> **Spacecraft finds dunes on Pluto**
>
> Scientists say that there are dunes of frozen methane on Pluto. A photo
> from a NASA mission to the dwarf planet shows wavy ridges, similar to
> satellite images of sand dunes on the Sahara Desert. The grains of
> methane are about the same size as grains of sand.
>
> Before the photo was taken, scientists knew that Pluto's winds are
> strong enough to blow methane grains around. But they also knew
> that the winds are not strong enough to lift methane grains off the
> surface in the first place.
>
> Having seen the photo, the scientists suggested how methane grains
> are lifted from the surface. Heat from the Sun makes the solid nitrogen
> on Pluto's surface sublime, they said. The nitrogen gas carries methane
> grains into the air.
>
> Other scientists are working on different ideas to explain how the
> methane dunes were formed.

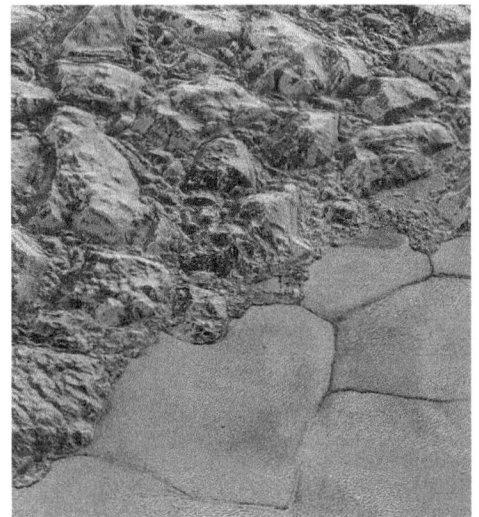

a Write down the NASA scientists' claim.

_____

b Write down **one** piece of evidence that supports the claim you identified in part **a**.

_____

c Write down **one** piece of evidence that does not support the claim.

_____

d In your opinion, which of the pieces of evidence is stronger – the one in your answer to part **b,** or the one in
your answer to part **c**?

_____

e Justify the opinion you gave in part **d**.

_____

_____

f Suggest an experiment that scientists could do on Earth to test the idea that subliming nitrogen lifts methane
grains into the air.

_____

_____

EP11 Risks and benefits

A Fill in the gaps to complete the sentences.

Every discovery or invention has risks and _____. Different people are affected by a new discovery

or invention in _____ ways. To make a decision, you need to weigh up the _____ and

benefits of a course of action.

B Wearable electronic fitness trackers were invented in the early 2000s. Now many people use them. Suggest benefits
and risks of electronic fitness trackers in the categories shown in the table.

Category	Benefits	Risks
People who wear fitness trackers		
The environment		

Hint: To help you to suggest risks and benefits, think about making, selling, and using fitness trackers.

C Different people have different opinions about fitness trackers. Suggest **one** reason for each of the opinions that is
given below.

a **Parent:** I think fitness trackers are brilliant. I bought one for my 13-year-old daughter, and am happy for her to
wear it all the time.

Suggested reason: _____

b **Headteacher:** I do not like fitness trackers. I have decided to ban them at my school.

Suggested reason: _____

c **Owner of company that makes fitness trackers:** Everyone should have a fitness tracker.

Suggested reason: _____

D Flu is a common infectious illness. If you have flu, you will probably have a high temperature, a headache, and a dry
cough. You will feel weak and exhausted. Most people who have flu make a full recovery, but some elderly people
and some people with respiratory ailments do not.

Every year, the British government provides free flu vaccinations for over-65s.

a Suggest **one** risk of vaccinating over-65s against flu.

_____

b Suggest **two** benefits of vaccinating over-65s against flu.

_____

_____

c Justify the decision to provide a free flu vaccination for over-65s.

_____

_____

_____

Hint: Refer to both risks and benefits in your answer.

EP12 Review theories 1

A Fill in the gaps to complete the sentences.

A theory is an _____ for patterns in observations or data that is supported by scientific

_____. For example, the behaviour of gases is explained by _____ theory. The origin of

the Universe is explained by the _____ _____ theory. Scientific theories have changed

over time, as scientists find new _____.

B **a** Tick the statements about scientific theories that are true.

    1 Most, but not all, scientific theories are supported by evidence. ☐

    2 Observations and data provide evidence for scientific theories. ☐

    3 Once scientists have decided on a theory, it does not change. ☐

    4 The theory of combustion has changed over time. ☐

    5 Observations of animals, plants, and fossils provide evidence for the theory of natural selection. ☐

    6 Scientists use theories to explain observations. ☐

    7 Scientists cannot use theories to make predictions. ☐

    8 Scientific theories are testable. ☐

  b Now write corrected versions of the **three** statements above that are not true.

_____

_____

_____

C A scientific theory explains patterns in observations and data. It also enables us to make predictions.

  a Complete column 2 in the table below by writing the name of one theory in each row.

    Choose from these theories: **Big Bang**, **evolution**, **kinetic**, **combustion**, **germ**

  b Complete column 3 by suggesting predictions that follow from the theories.

  Hint: Read part **b** carefully – it asks for predictions that follow from the **theories** (in the second column), **not** for predictions that follow from the **evidence** (in the first column).

Evidence	Theory that explains the evidence	Prediction that follows from the theory
Water vapour and air can occupy the same space at the same time.		
The Universe has been expanding for 14 billion years.		
Many people who collected water from the same pump in London became ill with cholera.		

D Compare the ways in which models and theories are used in science.

_____

_____

_____

_____

_____

_____

EP13 Review theories 2

A Fill in the gaps to complete the sentences.

If new evidence does not support an existing _____, a scientist may create a _____ theory to better explain the _____. The scientist will publish their ideas and discuss them at _____ to try to convince other scientists that the new theory is _____. Scientists can use a theory to make predictions, which can be _____. If the predictions are correct, more scientists will be convinced the theory is _____. The logical reasoning and debate are used to help refine a theory. This is called _____.

B Scientific theories change over time. Tick **one** box next to each statement in the table.

Statement	✔ This might provide a reason to change a scientific theory	✔ This increases the time for scientists to accept a new theory
a When microscopes were invented, scientists could see smaller objects in greater detail.		
b A scientist makes an observation that the old theory cannot explain.		
c Scientists are familiar with the old theory.		
d A new theory better predicts what will happen in new experiments.		
e Religious leaders might not accept new ideas that conflict with their beliefs.		
f Scientists collect new data that do not fit with the old theory.		

C Suggest suitable endings for the sentence starters below.

a Scientists might test a new theory by _____

_____

b A new theory might be wrong if _____

_____

c If scientists have looked for, but not found, evidence to contradict a theory, then _____

_____

Hint: If scientists find evidence that does not fit a certain scientific theory, the theory might be wrong.

D Argumentation is important in science.

a Define the meaning of argumentation.

_____

_____

b Explain why argumentation is important in science.

_____

c Suggest what might happen if scientists did not use argumentation as part of the process of developing scientific theories.

_____

_____

_____

Enquiry Processes Pinchpoint ⧓

Pinchpoint question

Answer the question below, then do the follow-up activity **with the same letter** as the answer you picked.

It takes a lot of debate, argumentation, and time for a new scientific theory to be accepted.

The main reason for this is…

A   it takes time for scientists to change their mind.

B   once a scientific theory is accepted, it becomes a scientific law.

C   it takes time for enough scientific evidence to be found.

D   that scientific theories are guesses made by scientists.

A Scientists changed from thinking that diseases were caused by bad air from rotting food to thinking that some diseases are transmitted by microorganisms (germ theory).

Fill in the gaps using the words in the box. You may use some of the words more than once.

bacteria	theory	evidence	germ theory	heat	diseases	antibiotic

It was generally thought that some diseases were caused by 'bad air'. Some scientists thought that these

diseases were spread by germs; this was called _____ _____. Over the years, more

_____ for germ theory was found. In the 1860s, Louis Pasteur found that _____

could be killed by _____. In the 1890s, Robert Koch found that different types of bacteria cause

different _____. This provided further _____ for the _____ that

microorganisms cause some diseases. Applying this _____, Alexander Fleming found that penicillin,

an _____, killed some bacteria and reduced the death rates from bacterial diseases. Scientists change

their minds when enough _____ supports the _____.

Hint: Think about why scientists changed from the bad air theory to germ theory. For help, see See EP12 Review theories 1 and EP13 Review theories 2.

B Draw one line to link each scientific idea to its definition.

a Scientific theory	**1** A statement that describes a phenomenon that always occurs under certain conditions. It does not offer an explanation about why it happens.
b Scientific law	**2** A scientific explanation for a pattern we see in observations or data. It is supported by scientific evidence and shown to be true through repeated experiments.
c Scientific model	**3** A way of representing something complex more simply. It helps explain the results of experiments or predict the outcome of experiments.

Hint: Make sure you know the difference between these keywords. For help, see EP6 More on planning how to answer a question and the Glossary.

C Advances in science and technology often allow scientific theories to be accepted.

Complete the table using the discoveries in the box.

Hubble telescope	discovery of antibiotics	discovery of DNA	splitting the atom

Scientific theory	Scientific advance that added evidence
Germ theory	
Theory of natural selection	
Kinetic theory	
The Big Bang theory	

Hint: When scientists make a technological discovery, the new evidence can support a scientific theory. For example, the development of microscopes provided evidence that cells existed. For help, see EP12 Review theories 1 and EP13 Review theories 2.

D Tick the features of a scientific theory.

1 It is supported by scientific evidence. ☐

2 It is the idea of a good scientist. ☐

3 It has been peer-reviewed by scientists. ☐

4 It is a best guess about a natural phenomenon. ☐

5 Experiments using the theory produce the same results (reproducible). ☐

6 It explains patterns based on scientific evidence. ☐

7 It sometimes changes if new scientific evidence is found. ☐

8 It is testable. ☐

Hint: A scientific theory is more than a good idea. For help, see EP12 Review theories 1 and EP13 Review theories 2.

1.3.1 Friction and drag

A Fill in the gaps to complete the sentences.

_____ grips objects because, although their surfaces might look smooth, they are actually

_____. One way to reduce friction is to use _____. Drag forces, such as

_____ resistance or _____ resistance, happen because an object has to push air or

water molecules out of the way. Making an object more _____ is a way to reduce drag. If no other

force is applied, friction and drag forces cause an object to _____ _____ or stop. Drag

and friction are examples of _____ forces, where the object affected must be touching the

substance causing the force.

The total of all the forces acting on an object is called the _____ force. If this is zero then the object

is in _____ – if it was stationary then it will stay _____, or if it was moving it will keep

moving with the _____ speed and _____.

The unit of force is the _____, symbol N.

B **a** A leaf falls from a tree. Initially it is moving very slowly and only one force is acting on the leaf.
Suggest which force this is.

_____

b As the leaf falls, it speeds up and another force acts on it, getting larger as it speeds up.
Suggest which other force is acting.

_____

c After a while, the two forces are equal and acting in opposite directions so that there is no resultant force.
Predict what will happen to the speed and direction of the leaf while it is still in the air.

_____

C For each question below, describe the change to each object's motion.

Explain in detail which forces cause each change and why they are acting.

a A boat is crossing a lake when the engine is cut.

_____

_____

_____

b A person pushing a box across a smooth wooden floor stops pushing.

_____

_____

_____

1.3.2 Squashing and stretching

A Fill in the gaps to complete the sentences.

Forces can change the shape of objects, or _____ them. Forces can _____ (squash) or stretch objects. When you stand on the floor, your weight compresses the bonds between the particles in the floor. They push back and the floor _____ up on you when you stand on it. This support force from the floor is called the _____ force. Bungee cords, springs, and even lift cables all _____ when you exert a force on them. The amount that they stretch is called the _____. A bungee cord will pull back on the person with a force called _____. Springs are special: if you double the force on a spring, the extension will _____. This relationship is called _____ and it is a _____ relationship. Beyond a particular force, the spring will not go back to its original length when you remove the force. This is the _____ limit.

Any graph that shows a straight line means there is a _____ relationship between the variables. A proportional relationship is a special kind of _____ relationship because the straight line goes through the _____ of the graph.

B A spring obeys Hooke's Law. It stretches by 1.2 cm when a force of 50 N is applied.
Calculate its extension when a force of 200 N is applied.

_____ cm

C Complete the table for each situation below, describing the effect on the object and giving an explanation for that effect. The first one is completed for you.

Situation	Description of effect on object	Explanation
Cushion supporting a person	Cushion is compressed	Weight of person pushes down, support force from cushion pushes up
Strap supporting a bag		
A bicycle tyre		

D Explain how a solid floor provides a support force to stop you falling towards the Earth. Use scientific terminology and the concept of bonding.

_____

_____

_____

_____

1.3.3 Turning forces

A Fill in the gaps to complete the sentences.

When we apply a force to a door that can _____ on its hinges, there is a turning effect called a

_____. The _____ of a force is defined and calculated as the _____

applied (N) times the perpendicular _____ to the _____ (m). It has the unit

_____ _____, symbol (N m). If a _____ of one newton is applied

one metre from a _____, then there is a _____ of one N m. If the sum of the

moments in a clockwise direction are equal to the sum of the moments in the anticlockwise direction, the object

is in _____ and it will not start turning. This is the _____ _____

_____. The centre of gravity (centre of mass) is the point through which the _____

appears to act. If the centre of gravity of an object is directly _____ or _____ the pivot

there will be _____ moment making it turn. If it is to the side of the pivot, the object will start to

_____ due to the moment.

B **a** Write down the equation for calculating moment of force.

_____

b Callum applies 5.0 N of force to a door handle 0.50 m from the hinges to open the door.
Calculate the moment of force.

_____

c Molly holds a 50 N bag of groceries. Her forearm is 0.40 m from her elbow to her hand.
Calculate the moment of force of the groceries about her elbow.

d Tightrope walkers must keep their centre of gravity directly above the rope.
Explain why this is important.

_____

_____

_____

C Fatima is trying to open a jar of jam. She has a problem with her hand and can only grip with a **force of 150 N**.
To help her open jars she uses a tool with a handle, such that the radius to the middle of her hand is increased to
110 mm. The jar requires a **moment of 10 N m** to open it.

a Rearrange the formula for calculating moment so that you can calculate force.

_____

b **i** Calculate the minimum force required to open the jar using the tool.

_____

ii Suggest whether she can now open it and why.

_____

14

1.4.1 Pressure in gases

A Fill in the gaps to complete the sentences.

A substance without a fixed shape, such as a gas or liquid, is called a _____. Gases, such as air, exert

_____ _____ because of collisions between the gas _____,

and between them and any surface they touch. When we squeeze a gas it is _____, which increases

its pressure and its _____.

Pressure is defined and calculated as the _____ applied (N) divided by the _____ over

which it is applied (m^2). It has the unit _____ _____ _____, symbol N/m^2.

If a _____ of one newton is applied over one square metre, there is a _____ of 1 N/m^2.

The air around us is at _____ _____, which causes a force pushing in on our skin. This

is balanced by the pressure from inside our bodies. As you go higher, such as up a mountain, _____

_____ gets _____.

B The photograph shows a pilot dressed to cope with the effects of being at high altitude.

Describe how atmospheric pressure changes with height and **one** effect this has on people.

_____

_____

_____

C La Paz is the highest-altitude capital city in the world, at 3640 m. At that altitude, atmospheric pressure is significantly lower, and therefore air is less dense.

Draw a line to match each effect with its cause.

| You can kick a football further because | | there is less oxygen per litre. |

| Athletes cannot run as far or as fast because | | neighbouring air particles collide with each other less often. |

| The speed of sound is lower because | | air particles collide with objects less often so there is less drag. |

D a Give the formula for calculating gas pressure.

_____

b A heavy-duty suction cup uses atmospheric pressure to lift heavy objects in a factory.

The cup has an area of 0.020 m^2 and atmospheric pressure is 100 000 N/m^2. Rearrange the formula for calculating fluid pressure to calculate the maximum force the suction cup can provide.

_____

1.4.2 Pressure in liquids

A Fill in the gaps to complete the sentences.

Liquids, such as water, exert _____ _____ because of how the particles push against

each other and anything they touch. There is a difference in _____ between the top and bottom

of an object which is in water. This causes a force called _____. This is what causes people to float

when they are swimming. When liquids are squeezed their _____ hardly changes at all: they are

_____.

B Complete each diagram to show the forces on each object.

   a   A boat floating.

   b   An anchor about to sink.

C Water pressure is very different deep in the ocean compared to near the surface. Explain how and why it is different, using each of these keywords at least once: **pressure**, **deeper**, **weight**

_____

_____

_____

_____

D A simple hydraulic machine uses fluid pressure to multiply force.

   a **i** Recall the equation to calculate fluid pressure.

_____

      ii The user pushes down with a force of 40 N on the smaller piston, which has an area of 0.40 m². Calculate the pressure in the fluid.

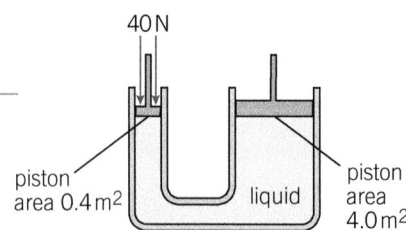

40 N

piston area 0.4 m²   liquid   piston area 4.0 m²

   b Pressure is the same throughout the fluid, including at the larger piston which has an area of 4.0 m². Rearrange the formula for pressure to calculate the force that the fluid exerts on the piston.

1.4.3 Stress on solids

A Fill in the gaps to complete the sentences.

Stress is defined and calculated as the _____ applied (N) divided by the _____

_____ over which it is applied (m²). It has the unit _____ _____

_____ _____, symbol N/m². If a _____ of one newton is applied

over one square metre, there is a _____ of 1 N/m². A large force exerted on a small area exerts

a _____ stress on the surface, whereas the same force spread over a larger area will result in

_____ stress on the surface.

B a Write down the equation for calculating stress.

_____

b A box of cereal has a weight of 5.0 N, and an area of 0.010 m².
Calculate the stress it exerts on its kitchen shelf.

_____

c A garden shed and its foundations have a weight of 2500 N, and an area of 6.4 m².
Calculate the stress it exerts on the ground.

_____

C Bobby is skiing across country. To avoid sinking into the snow, the stress under his skis should not exceed 2800 N/m².
He has a mass of 78 kg.

a Calculate Bobby's weight. The gravitational field strength is 10 N/kg.

_____

b Rearrange the equation for stress to calculate the minimum area required for his skis.

_____

D a The Canadian lynx and the bobcat are related species of large cat that live in North America. They are both of a
similar size and body mass. The lynx lives where there is often deep snow in winter and the bobcat lives where
there is little snow.

Suggest why the lynx has much larger paws than the bobcat.

_____

_____

b A drawing pin has a sharp point, and a large head to make it easier to push the pin into a surface.

Explain why the point needs to be sharp but the head needs to be large.

_____

_____

Pinchpoint question

Answer the question below, then do the follow-up activity **with the same letter** as the answer you picked.

A chair is on the floor of a room. Choose the best explanation of how the floor supports it.

A   The chair has weight, so it is exerting a force downwards on the floor. This compresses the bonds between the particles making up the floor. The compressed bonds exert a force back on the chair, stopping it falling through the floor.

B   Only living animals can push anything – the floor only pushes up on the chair when a person sits on it and pushes it down. The floor then pushes back with an equal and opposite force, holding the chair up.

C   The chair has weight. The floor pushes back up on the chair with the weight of the floor, using the force of gravity, as both the chair and the floor have mass. This holds the chair up.

D   The floor compresses the particles making up the chair. This causes the compressed particles in the chair to push down on the floor with a reaction force. This pushes the floor away from the chair.

Follow-up activities

A The photograph shows a crane lifting a heavy object.

   a   Describe what happens to the length of the cable supporting the load, and explain this in terms of the particles in the cable.

   _____

   _____

   _____

   _____

   _____

   _____

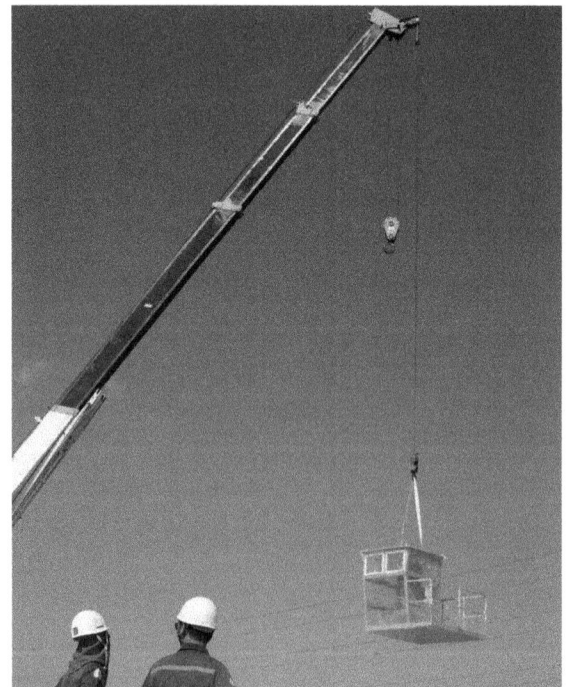

   b   The cable in the crane is found to obey Hooke's law.
      When a force of 3.0 kN is applied, there is an extension of 2.0 cm.
      Calculate the force that will cause an extension of 5.0 cm.

   _____

Hint: Are the forces compressing or tensing the cable? For help, see 1.3.2 Squashing and stretching.

B Many objects – living and non-living – have forces acting on them all the time.

a Tick which statement about weight (the force of gravity) is true.

1 It acts on any object with mass no matter where it is in the Universe, even far from stars and planets. ☐

2 It acts on any object that has mass if it is near something that has a lot of mass, such as the Earth. ☐

3 It acts only when a person provides a push. ☐

b Describe what will happen to a stationary object that has balanced forces (no resultant force) acting on it.

_____

c Draw and label on the diagram the forces acting on this building.

Hint: Which forces are acting on most stationary objects on Earth? For help, see 1.1.2 Balanced and unbalanced.

C a For each force, tick which descriptions apply.

Description	Weight (gravity)	Reaction force
Contact force		
Non-contact force		
Acts when mass is near a large mass such as the Earth		
Acts when one object is pushed against another		

b Draw and label on the diagram the forces acting on this building. There are two forces acting, one of which is weight (gravity).

Hint: What kind of force is gravity? For help, see 1.1.1 Introduction to forces.

D Forces are often due to the interaction between two objects. When discussing them, it is very important to be clear which object is acting, and which has the force acting on it.

  a On the diagram below, draw and label an arrow to represent the reaction force from the **building** acting on the **ground**. Then, draw and label an arrow to represent the reaction force from the **ground** acting on the **building.**

  b Use these keywords to complete these sentences about the forces between the building and the ground, to explain why the building does not fall into the ground.

particles	particles	compressed	building	building	opposite
bonds	ground	bonds	equal	ground	push

When a force acts on an object, the _____ between the _____ it consists of are

_____, squeezing the particles closer together. The particles then _____ back, causing

the object to push back with a force that is _____ in size and in the _____ direction.

The building does not fall through the ground because the _____ acts on the _____

with a force. Both the building and ground act on each other, compressing the _____ between

_____ in both of them. However, it is the force from the _____ acting on the

_____ that matters.

Hint: Which forces are acting on most stationary objects on Earth? For help, see 1.1.2 Balanced and unbalanced and 1.3.2 Squashing and stretching.

Pinchpoint review
Now look back at the question – do you think you chose the right letter?
Turn to the Answers page to find out.

A Fill in the gaps to complete the sentences.

Some materials are attracted to a magnet , or can be themselves turned into permanent _____ .

These are called _____ _____ , and include the elements _____, nickel,

and cobalt, and some types of steel, which contains _____. Every magnet has a _____

_____ and a _____ _____ . A compass is a magnet that is free to rotate.

It will spin until its _____ pole points to the _____ magnetic North Pole, which is

actually a magnetic _____ pole.

Two magnets will attract each other if they have _____ poles nearest to each other, or repel

if they have the _____ poles nearest to each other. We say that magnets are surrounded by a

_____ _____, which we can detect using a compass or iron filings. We can represent

this by drawing _____ _____ _____, which point from the north pole

to the south pole, and show where a field is strong by drawing _____ of them. The field causes a

magnetic _____ .

B For each combination of magnets below, write whether they will attract, repel, or have no effect.

a | N | | S | _____
b | S | | N | _____
c | N | | N | _____
d | S | | S | _____

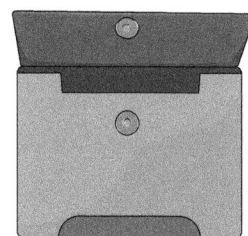

C It is possible to use a pair of magnets as a fastener on a bag. People with limited mobility in their hands can find these fasteners particularly easy to use.

Explain how two magnets can be used to hold a bag closed.

_____

_____

D **a** Complete the diagram below to show the magnetic field lines around a bar magnet.

  b On your diagram for part **a**, add two labels to the magnetic field:

- **W** to show a weaker part of the field.

| N | | S |

- **S** to show a stronger part of the field.

E Lara is a physicist who needs to find which direction is north.

Describe how she can use a magnet to do so.

_____

_____

_____

2.4.1 Electromagnets

A Fill in the gaps to complete the sentences.

An electromagnet consists of a _____ of wire with many _____, wrapped around a _____. To make an electromagnet stronger, create _____ _____ on the coil, use a larger _____, or use a _____ in the core that is easy to _____, such as iron. Electromagnets can be more useful than _____ magnets because they can be _____ _____ or made far stronger. The magnetic _____ around an electromagnet is very similar to that around a _____ magnet. Another name for a coil is a _____.

B Fill in the gaps using these keywords to explain how an electromagnet works. You may use the keywords once, more than once, or not at all.

core	field	doesn't	current
magnetic material	magnetic field	coil	does

An electromagnet consists of a _____ passing through a _____ of wire, usually wrapped around an iron _____. This creates a _____ _____. If the _____ is switched off then the electromagnet _____ pick up magnetic material.

C Describe **two** ways to make an electromagnet stronger.

_____

_____

D A physicist carries out a set of experiments on the strength of an electromagnet by making the following changes.

- Decrease number of turns on coil
- Reverse direction of current

For each variable she changes, predict and explain whether the strength of the electromagnet will become weaker, become stronger, or stay the same.

_____

_____

_____

_____

E Anna places two wires carrying current parallel to each other. She wonders whether each will act on the other with a magnetic force.

Suggest whether you think there will be a force, and give a reason.

_____

_____

2.4.2 Using electromagnets

A Fill in the gaps to complete the sentences.

In an electric bell, when a switch is closed, _____ passes through a _____, making an electromagnet. The coil attracts an _____ armature, which then breaks the circuit. The repeated making and breaking of the circuit rings the _____.

A circuit breaker has an _____ armature completing the circuit, which is held in place with springs. When the _____ in a nearby _____ becomes too large, the magnetic field created attracts the armature out of place and breaks the circuit. It is designed to protect the devices from power surges and to protect people from electric shocks.

A loudspeaker depends on a varying _____ in a _____ causing a varying magnetic field which attracts and repels a permanent _____, moving the cone of the loudspeaker in and out.

B Reorder the statements below to describe how a loudspeaker works.

Correct order: ☐ ☐ ☐ ☐

1 Current flows in coil.
2 Connect coil to the power source.
3 Coil becomes an electromagnet.
4 Forces between the coil and the permanent magnet make the cone move.

C You are provided with a long piece of wire, a 10-cm-long iron bar, a cell, and a switch.
Describe how you would use these items to separate magnetic materials in a model recycling plant.
Include a circuit diagram in your answer and explain why a switch is essential.

_____
_____
_____
_____

D Give **one** similarity and **one** difference between the ways in which an electric bell and a circuit breaker use electromagnetism.
Similarity:
_____
_____

Difference:
_____
_____

E Elijah is an engineer. He is designing a circuit breaker. He has chosen to double the number of turns on the coil.
Circle the keywords to suggest what effect this will have.

The coil acts as an **energy source / electromagnet** when the current flows. Doubling the number of turns creates a **weaker / stronger** magnetic field, so makes the electromagnet **stronger / weaker**. In a circuit breaker, this triggers the device at a **lower / higher** current, making the device **more / less** sensitive.

Big Idea 2 Pinchpoint ⊗

Pinchpoint question

Answer the question below, then do the follow-up activity **with the same letter** as the answer you picked.

The diagrams show two devices that use electromagnetism: an electric bell and a loudspeaker.

Choose the option that best compares and contrasts how these devices work.

A Both use a current that does not change; the speaker is supplied from a music source and the bell is supplied by a battery for as long as the switch is pushed.

B Both involve a current in a coil causing it to become an electromagnet; the speaker pushes against a permanent magnet, and the bell pulls on a strip of iron.

Electric bell   Loudspeaker

C Both use an electrical force from the coil on another component; the speaker pushes against a diaphragm (cone), and the bell pulls on a strip of metal.

D Both involve the circuit automatically being completed and broken repeatedly, for as long as the device is on: this makes the speaker diaphragm (cone) send one sound wave each time or makes the bell ring once each time.

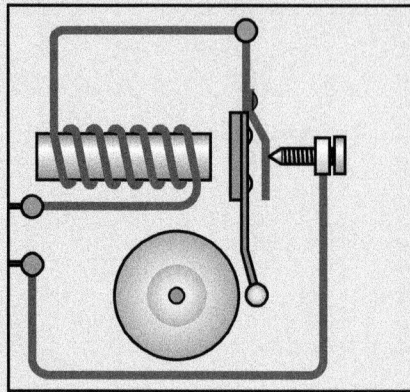

Follow-up activities

A a Write the order of statements that gives the best explanation of what happens when the electric bell rings.

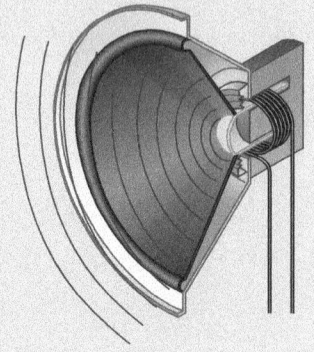

Correct order: ☐ ☐ ☐ ☐ ☐ ☐

1 The springy metal strip pushes back, so the bell rings.

2 That breaks the circuit, stopping the current.

3 The iron armature is attracted to the coil.

4 The circuit is complete again, so the whole process begins again.

5 There is current in the coil, so it acts as an electromagnet.

6 The electromagnet no longer provides a magnetic force.

b To emit a sound wave, the diaphragm (cone) of the speaker must move backwards and forwards. Explain how this is caused, using each of the keywords below at least once.

coil	electromagnet	magnetic force
	permanent magnet	varying current

Hint: What causes the bell to ring repeatedly? For help, see 2.4.2 Using electromagnets.

B Another device that uses electromagnetism is a magnetic door lock, as shown in the diagram.

Suggest how electromagnetism can be used to unlock the door.

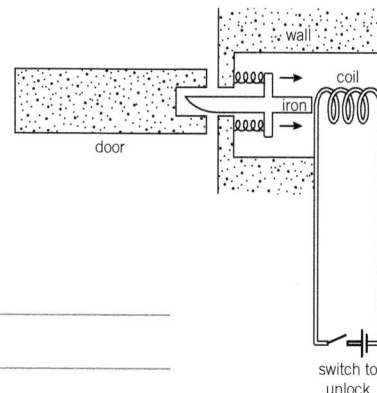

_____

_____

_____

_____

Hint: Which components might be similar to those in a loudspeaker? For help, see 2.4.2 Using electromagnets.

C a Tick which force each description applies to.

Description	Electric force	Magnetic force
Contact force		
Non-contact force		
Acts between charges		
Acts between magnetic materials or currents		

b Complete the sentences below using the keywords in the box.

electromagnet	magnetic	magnetic	diaphragm (cone)	current
magnet	magnetic	magnetic	iron	armature breaks	coil

In both devices, a _____ in a coil turns it into an _____.

In a loudspeaker, the _____ field from this acts on a permanent _____.

The _____ force pushes the _____ backwards and forwards, moving a _____.

In an electric bell, the _____ field from this acts on a piece of _____.

The _____ force pulls the _____ so that the bell rings and the circuit _____.

Hint: What are some differences between electric and magnetic fields? For help, see 2.2.2 Charging up and 2.3.1 Magnets and magnetic fields.

D Each statement below contains a mistake. Rewrite each to give a correct explanation for how a **loudspeaker** works.

a Current in the coil makes it into a permanent magnet.

_____

b The electric force from the permanent magnet onto the coil depends on the current.

_____

c The loudspeaker is supplied with a constant direct current all the time the speaker is making a sound.

_____

d The varying current causes the coil, and therefore the diaphragm (cone), to stay still.

_____

Hint: What kind of current is supplied to loudspeakers? For help, see 2.4.2 Using electromagnets.

Pinchpoint review

Now look back at the question – do you think you chose the right letter?
Turn to the Answers page to find out.

3.3.1 Work, energy, and machines

A Fill in the gaps to complete the sentences.

When an object is moved by a force through a distance, for instance if we deform a spring, we say that _____ is done. The distance moved in a straight line from its starting point is also called its _____. It is a way of transferring _____, like heating. Work _____ is defined and calculated as the force (N) times the distance moved in direction of force (m). It has the same unit as energy, the _____, symbol J. If a _____ of one newton moves an object one metre, then one joule of _____ is done, and one joule of _____ is transferred between stores. Some devices can reduce the force you need to apply to move an object, so that the output force is _____ than the input force. Other devices can increase the distance the object moves when you apply a force. All such devices are called _____ _____. Examples include _____, pulleys, and _____.

B A mechanic applies a force of 120 N to a lever to lift a car, moving the lever through a distance of 0.40 m. Calculate the work he does on the lever.

C A machine that lifts a load to place it on a shelf in a warehouse is operated by a foot pump.

A load of 1500 N needs to be raised by 1.0 m.

a Calculate the work done if Ethan lifts that load himself.

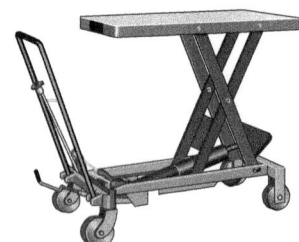

b Lifting the load 1.0 m requires 30 presses of the foot pump, each needing Ethan to do 50 J of work (ignoring the effect of friction).

Calculate the work done by Ethan using the machine.

c Explain how the principle of conservation of energy applies to Ethan lifting the load by 1.0 m using the lift table, using each of these keywords at least once.

chemical store	gravitational store	thermal store	equal	fills	empties

3.4.1 Energy and temperature

A Fill in the gaps to complete the sentences.

We describe how hot or cold something is as its _____. We measure this using a

_____, using the unit of _____ _____, symbol _____.

If a hotter object is put in contact with a colder one, the hot one will heat the cold one until they reach

the _____ temperature and are in _____, that is, until _____

_____ energy is transferred between their _____ energy stores.

The energy that you need to raise the temperature of a material depends on the _____ of material

and the _____ of material, as well as on how much you want to raise the temperature.

B **a** When an object is heated, both its temperature and the energy in its thermal energy store increase.
   Use the words in the list below to complete the following sentences about temperature and energy.

increases J °C move / vibrate thermal increases stays the same

   Temperature is measured in _____. As we increase the mass of an object, for instance by adding

   more water to a glass, its temperature _____. As temperature _____, the particles

   that make up the object _____ more.

   Energy is measured in _____. As the mass of the object increases, the amount of energy in its

   _____ energy store _____.

 b Circle the correct **bold** words to complete the following sentence about heat and thermal energy.

   The amount of energy in the thermal store of a glass of water is **less than / the same as / more than** in

   a swimming pool at the same temperature.

C Suggest and explain which you expect to have a larger thermal store of energy: one cubic metre of water or one
cubic metre of air at the same temperature.

_____

_____

D For each of the following situations, explain whether equilibrium has been reached.

 a A person outside shivering in the cold.

_____

 b A cup of tea that has been left in a room overnight.

_____

 c A thermometer in a patient's mouth for a minute.

_____

A Fill in the gaps to complete the sentences.

Energy can be transferred by heating – this transfers the energy from a _____ energy store

associated with a _____ object into the thermal store of a _____ object. This can

happen in three ways. Particles in a hot material _____. When they collide with their neighbours,

making them vibrate, we call that thermal _____. This process happens fastest with materials in a

_____ state and slowest with materials in a _____ state. Materials where this happens

very slowly are called thermal _____.

When you heat a liquid or gas, its particles move further apart so the fluid becomes less _____.

The hotter, less _____ fluid then rises, moving to a place that is colder. The colder, denser fluid then

_____ and the process is repeated. This process is called _____. The movement of the

fluid from one place to another is called a _____ _____.

B The image shows a pan of soup being heated on a stove, with the soup moving because of convection.

Reorder these statements to explain the process of convection.

Correct order: ☐ ☐ ☐ ☐

1 Particles in a heated liquid move further apart, so the liquid expands.

2 The lower density liquid moves upwards through colder liquid.

3 The more dense colder liquid sinks and is then heated at the base of the pan.

4 The soup at the bottom of the pan is heated, and its particles move and vibrate faster.

C Fill in the gaps using the keywords below to explain why certain materials are good thermal insulators.

solids	gases	thermal	weak	air	far apart	non-metals

_____ are good _____ insulators because their particles are _____

_____, with _____ forces between them. Some _____ are also good

insulators such as many _____, like wood and certain plastics. Many of the best insulators are solids

that trap little pockets of _____.

D Lexi carries out an experiment to see which cup is best at keeping drinks cold. She measures the time it takes for
a cold drink to warm by 10 °C. To make it a fair test, all the cups contained the same volume of liquid at the same
starting temperature, had the same colour and finish on the outside, and the same lid. The table shows her results.

Cup	Time to warm by 10 °C (hours)
Tough, solid, steel	0.5
Expanded polystyrene foam	3.0
Two layers of plastic separated by a vacuum	6.0

Use your knowledge of thermal insulators and conductors to explain the result for the **best** insulator.

_____

_____

_____

3.4.3 Energy transfer: radiation and insulation

A Fill in the gaps to complete the sentences.

To transfer thermal energy by _____ or _____ requires particles. However, these

are not needed for heating by _____. Hot objects emit _____ _____,

sometimes known as thermal radiation or heat. This can be detected using a _____

_____ _____, for instance to help firefighters find people in a smoke-filled room. When

objects _____ this radiation, they warm up. It is a wave like light and can be _____,

_____, or _____. Surfaces that have a _____ colour and

_____ finish absorb infrared better than ones that are _____ and _____.

B a Draw a line to match each method of energy transfer with its cause.

Conduction	Emission and absorption of infrared
Convection	Particles moving from a hotter place to a colder place
Radiation	In solids, particles vibrating and colliding with neighbours

b Explain how energy is transferred by radiation using these keywords:

radiation	emit	absorb	infrared	hot objects	heating

_____

_____

_____

_____

c Suggest one piece of evidence that radiation does not need particles to transfer energy.

_____

Hint: What do you feel when you turn your face to the Sun?

C The photograph shows a 'heat sink' used to cool computer components. It has a dull surface.

Explain how the heat sink works.

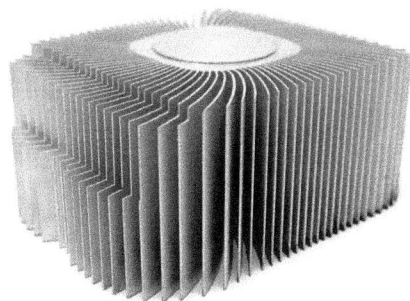

_____

_____

_____

_____

Hint: Why does it have this shape and finish?

Pinchpoint question

Answer the question below, then do the follow-up activity **with the same letter** as the answer you picked.

Rory is gently heating a pan of soup and wonders why, even without stirring it, the soup starts moving around the pan as shown in the diagram.

Choose the best explanation.

A The particles of the soup at the bottom of the pan are moving faster, so they move further apart. This means the hot soup at the bottom of the pan is less dense and floats to the top.

B The particles making up the soup do not move from one place to another: they knock into their neighbouring particles and pass on their energy that way.

C Heat rises: heat acts like a substance, and it rises taking the soup with it.

D The particles of the soup at the bottom of the pan have expanded as they got hotter, so the hot soup at the bottom of the pan is less dense and floats to the top.

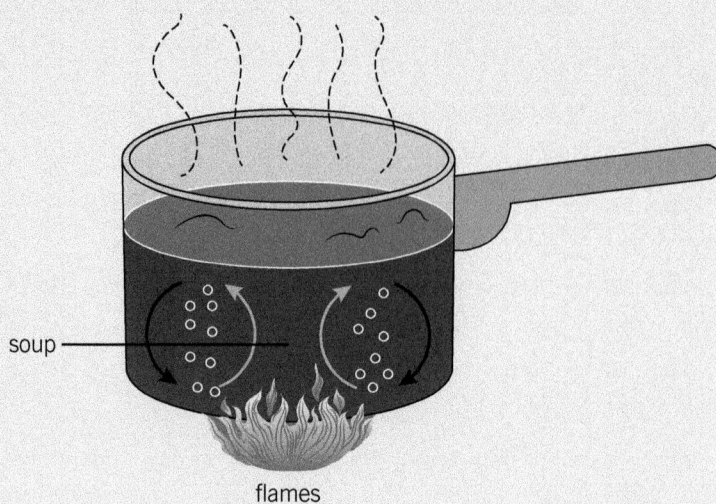

soup

flames

A Fans cause forced convection and are one way of cooling a hot object, by causing a flow of air over its surface.

A fan for cooling a person

A power unit for a computer, with a built-in cooling fan

They are used by people in warm weather, and for computer components. They are more effective at cooling than free convection, when the air is allowed to move naturally.

Use your knowledge of energy transfers to suggest why forced convection is more effective.

_____

_____

_____

_____

Hint: Why does convection transfer energy away from the hotter object? For help, see 3.4.2 Energy transfer: particles.

B There are three methods of energy transfer by heating. Convection is the most important in the example in the Pinchpoint question.

Identify each diagram as radiation, conduction, or convection, and give a brief description of how the thermal energy is transferred in each process.

Diagram	Energy transfer method	Description
thermal store at a high temperature thermal store at a low temperature		

Hint: What are the differences between methods of energy transfer? For help, see 3.4.2 Energy transfer: particles and 3.4.3 Energy transfer: radiation and insulation.

C An important scientific model of the world is that things are made of matter, which consists of particles. Energy is a way of describing what is happening to these particles.

Reorder the following statements to explain why the soup moves.

Correct order: ☐ ☐ ☐ ☐ ☐ ☐

1 When it is heated, the particles move past each other and vibrate more quickly.

2 The particles move further apart.

3 The density of the soup closer to the heat source is now lower than the colder soup higher up in the saucepan.

4 Soup is a liquid that is made of particles.

5 The hot, low-density soup floats up, moving past the colder, high-density soup, which sinks.

6 This movement is called a convection current.

Hint: What is the scientific explanation of convection? For help, see 3.4.2 Energy transfer: particles.

D The particles making up a liquid do not change in size.

a Use these keywords to complete the sentences about changing state.

gas	arranged	liquid	liquid	particles	solid

If some ice is heated, it melts first from a _____ to a _____. Then, if heating

continues, it boils, changing from a _____ to a _____. In each case, the

_____ themselves have not changed, just how they are _____ within the

substance.

b Similarly, if a liquid expands on heating, it is not that its particles themselves have changed. They have just moved further apart, making the substance as a whole expand.

Sketch below how a few of the particles are arranged in a cold liquid and in a hot liquid.

cold liquid

hot liquid

Hint: How are the particles in a liquid arranged? For help, see 3.4.1 Energy and temperature.

⊗ **Pinchpoint review**

Now look back at the question – do you think you chose the right letter?
Turn to the Answers page to find out.

4.3.1 Sound waves, water waves, and energy

A Fill in the gaps to complete the sentences.

In a sound wave, there are places where air particles are squeezed closer together, called _____,

and other places where they are further apart, called _____. Therefore, sound is a

_____ wave. A device that converts a sound wave into an electrical signal is called a

_____. A device that converts an electrical signal into a sound wave is a _____.

A sound that has a frequency higher than humans can hear, above _____ Hz, is called

_____.

B a Using the keywords below, describe how a microphone detects sound and converts it into an electrical signal.

diaphragm	sound wave	vibrate	coil	potential difference

_____

_____

b Explain how a loudspeaker and a microphone use changes in air pressure and potential difference.

_____

_____

C Read the following paragraph and circle the correct **bold** words below to describe why ultrasound is used rather than sound.

Ultrasound can be used for cleaning objects. They are put in water into which high-power ultrasound waves are emitted. Higher-frequency ultrasound is more effective for cleaning small parts and fine details.

The ultrasound waves vibrate the water particles at a **lower / higher** frequency than sound waves, cleaning the object more effectively.

The ultrasound has a wavelength that is **lower / higher** than for sound, so that the areas cleaned best are closer together.

D Two locations in Scotland, UK are being considered to build a power station that uses wave power.

Choose the best location and justify your choice using the information in the table.

Location name	Location type	Average wave height (m)
Lossiemouth	East coast, mainland	1.1
Breanais	West coast of an island	2.6

_____

_____

4.3.2 Radiation and energy

A Fill in the gaps to complete the sentences.

The _____ _____ consists of seven sections of waves, each with different properties.

We can only see the _____ _____ section; the rest are all invisible.

All are emitted by the _____. Each section has a characteristic range of _____

and frequencies. Gamma rays at one end of the spectrum have a _____ frequency, carry

_____ energy, and have a short _____. Radio waves at the other end have a

_____ frequency, carry _____ energy, and have a _____ wavelength.

Ultra violet, X-rays, and _____ rays all carry enough energy to remove an electron from an atom and

_____ it. This can cause _____ in human cells. Infrared and _____ carry

less energy and cause a heating effect.

B Name **two** wave bands of the electromagnetic spectrum that cannot be seen with the naked eye and give a use for each.

Band 1 _____ Use _____

Band 2 _____ Use _____

C a Fill in the names of the parts of the electromagnetic spectrum below, from short wavelength to long wavelength.

short wavelength ──────────────────────────────→ long wavelength

b Add a similar arrow and label above to show which end of the spectrum has **high frequency**.

D a Microwave ovens and mobile phones do not cause ionisation, whereas hospital X-ray machines do.

Explain why only some electromagnetic waves cause ionisation.

_____

_____

_____

_____

Hint: What is the link between the frequency of a wave and the energy it transfers?

b Reorder these statements to give the best explanation of how X-rays can cause harm to living cells.

Correct order: ☐ ☐ ☐ ☐

1 DNA in cell is ionised

2 Damaged DNA can cause mutation

3 Mutation might produce cancer

4 X-ray absorbed by cell

4.4.1 Modelling waves

A Fill in the gaps to complete the sentences.

In science, a _____ is an oscillation or vibration that transfers _____ or information.

In a _____ wave, the oscillation is at 90° to the direction of travel of the wave. In a _____

wave, the oscillation is parallel to the direction of travel of the wave. When a wave travels through a medium it is

called _____. When waves are put together they _____ – they add up or cancel out.

B A slinky spring can be used to demonstrate many aspects of wave behaviour.

Describe how it can model:

a reflection: _____

_____

b transmission: _____

_____

c absorption: _____

_____

C a Give **one** similarity and **one** difference between transverse and longitudinal waves.

Similarity: _____

Difference: _____

b Give **one** example of each type of wave.

Transverse: _____

Longitudinal: _____

D a When waves from two light sources combine, sometimes dark spots can be seen. Using the concept of superposition, suggest why this might happen.

_____

_____

b Harriet is a physicist considering two models for a light wave, as shown in the diagrams.

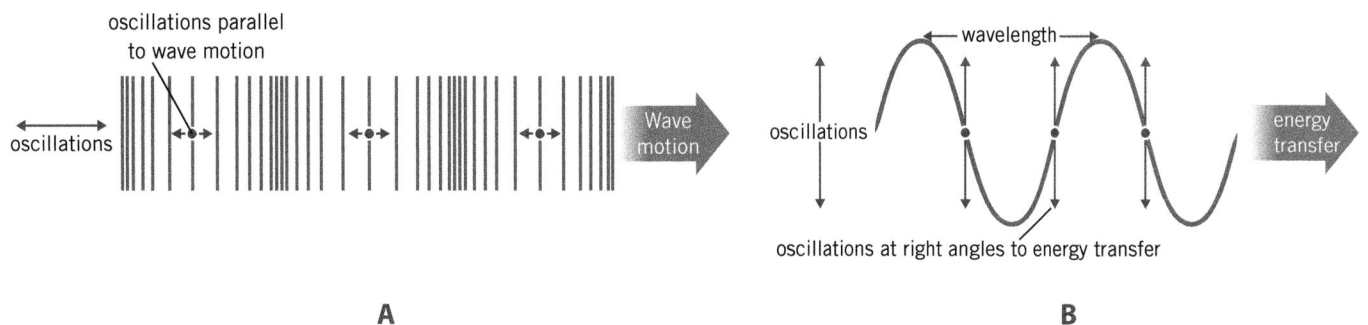

oscillations parallel to wave motion

oscillations

Wave motion

A

wavelength

oscillations

oscillations at right angles to energy transfer

energy transfer

B

Identify which model is the more suitable and give a reason for your choice.

_____

_____

Big Idea 4 Pinchpoint ⊗

Pinchpoint question

Answer the question below, then do the follow-up activity with the same letter as the answer you picked.

Annabelle is analysing the motion of the ground during a recent earthquake. The diagram shows how the ground shifted while a disturbance moved in the direction of the arrow.

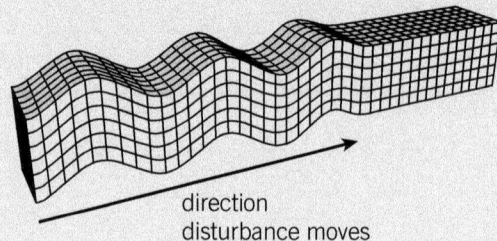

She is wondering whether a transverse wave is a good model for this phenomenon.

Select the best answer below.

direction
disturbance moves

A   No, it is not a good model. In a wave, particles travel the whole length of the wave. However, no part of the ground moved that far – each part just oscillated around one place.

B   No, it is not a good model. In a transverse wave, the oscillation is parallel to the direction of the wave. However, here the ground oscillated at right angles to the direction the wave moved.

C   Yes, it is a good model. Waves do not transfer energy, and no energy was transferred during the earthquake.

D   Yes, it is a good model. In transverse waves, energy is transferred at right angles to the direction of the oscillations.

Follow-up activities

A   A transverse wave consists of a series of oscillations, which move along the wave.

   a   Fill in the labels on the diagram using these keywords.

wavelength	energy transfer	oscillations

   b   Describe how the direction of movement of the particles in the spring relates to the direction of energy transfer.

   _____

   _____

   Hint: What direction are the oscillations in a wave? For help, see 4.4.1 Modelling waves.

B   **a**   This diagram shows a sound wave, which is a longitudinal wave.

   Describe how the motion of the air particles compares to the motion of the wave.

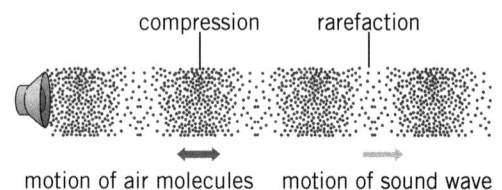

   compression   rarefaction

   motion of air molecules   motion of sound wave

   _____

   _____

b This diagram shows a water wave, which is a transverse wave, moving to the right.

Describe how the motion of the water particles compares to the motion of the wave.

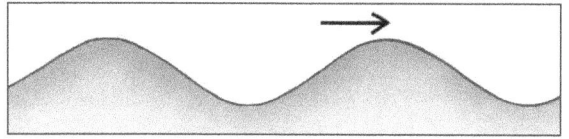

_____

_____

Hint: What is the difference between a transverse and a longitudinal wave? For help, see 4.4.1 Modelling waves.

C a Fill in the gaps to complete the sentences about energy and work.

Work done is defined as _____ times _____. If 1 J of work is done then

_____ J of energy must have been _____ between energy stores. Changing the

shape of an object requires applying a _____ and pushing it through a _____.

Destroying a building means that _____ was done and _____ was required.

b Complete the sentences about energy transfer using these keywords.

gamma ray	infrared	turbine	ionise	water waves

Electricity can be generated by _____ _____, because they transfer energy while

moving a _____. _____ radiation heats an object when it is absorbed.

A _____ _____ transfers enough energy to _____ an atom,

removing an electron from it.

Hint: Which kinds of waves can transfer energy? For help, see 4.3.1 Sound waves, water waves, and energy, and 4.3.2 Radiation and energy.

D The diagram shows two types of waves that occur during earthquakes. These can only travel along the surface of the Earth and appear after P- and S-waves.

Love wave

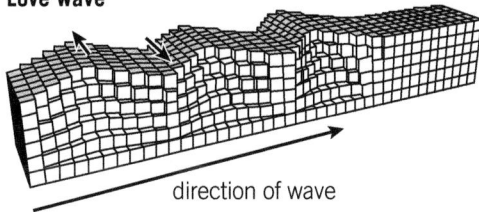

direction of wave

Rayleigh wave

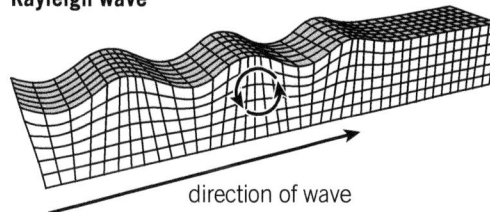

direction of wave

Suggest what happens to a structure such as a road or house when one of these waves reaches it.

_____

_____

⊗ **Pinchpoint review**
Now look back at the question – do you think you chose the right letter?
Turn to the Answers page to find out.

Section 1 Revision questions

1 🧪🧪 In 2006, Hannah McKeand set the record for reaching the South Pole in the fastest time.

In one hour she travelled approximately 3000 m pulling a sledge of food and equipment requiring a force of 200 N.

Calculate the work she did in one hour and give the unit of work. *(2 marks)*

_____

2 🧪🧪 The pressure of a gas is important; for instance, air pressure helps us to predict the weather.

  a Tick the variables that affect the pressure of a gas. *(2 marks)*

   1 temperature   ☐
   2 electrical charge   ☐
   3 volume   ☐
   4 distance   ☐

  b Give the formula for calculating pressure. *(1 mark)*

  _____

  c Sometimes people get stuck in thick mud by rivers. A problem for firefighters when they rescue them is avoiding get stuck themselves. A firefighter has a large board to stand on, which measures 1.8 m long and 0.50 m wide.

   i Calculate the area of the board. *(1 mark)*

   _____

   ii The firefighter has a weight of 800 N. Calculate the pressure he will exert when standing on the board and include the unit. *(2 marks)*

   _____

   iii If the pressure on the ground is above 20 000 N/m², the firefighter will sink into the mud. Explain whether he will sink if he stands on the board. *(1 mark)*

   _____
   _____

3 🧪🧪 Waves can be either transverse or longitudinal.

  a Describe the difference between transverse and longitudinal waves. *(2 marks)*

  _____
  _____
  _____
  _____

  b A physicist is investigating the relationship between frequency and wavelength for sound waves in air. Plot the data in **Table 1** on the graph paper below, with frequency on the *x*-axis and wavelength on the *y*-axis, and draw a line of best fit. *(3 marks)*

Table 1

Frequency (Hz)	Wavelength (m)
40	8.6
60	5.7
80	4.3
120	2.9
160	2.1
240	1.4
320	1.1

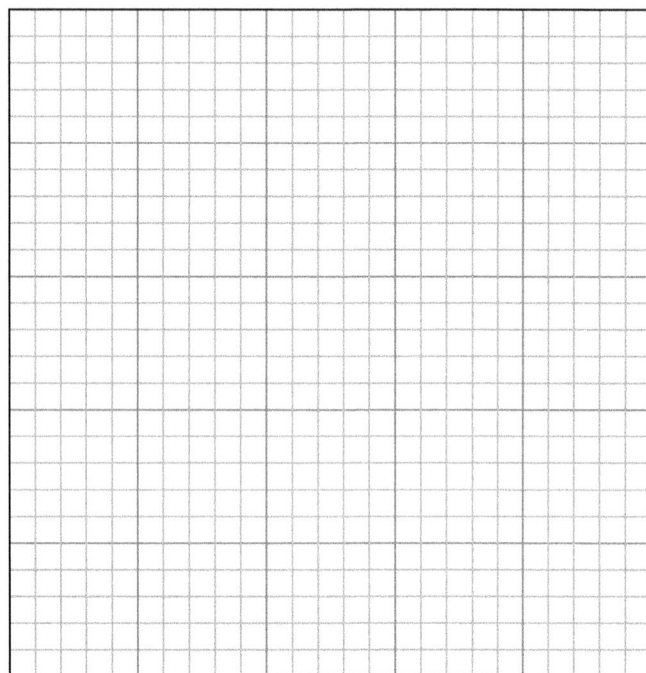

4 🧪🧪 Endurance athletes, such as marathon runners, are often handed a thin, shiny blanket as they cross the finishing line.

Suggest which form of energy transfer this is mainly designed to reduce and how it does so. *(2 marks)*

_____
_____
_____

5 ⚗️⚗️ Current in a wire acts as an electromagnet.

a Circle the option below that shows how the magnetic field strength varies with distance from the wire. *(1 mark)*

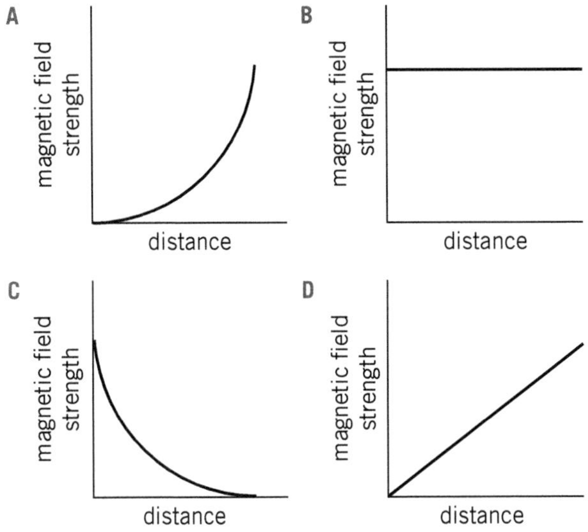

A | B

C | D

b The loudspeaker in a pair of earphones uses electromagnetism to play music from a phone. Describe how a loudspeaker works. Draw a labelled diagram to help your description. *(6 marks)*

_____

_____

_____

_____

_____

_____

_____

_____

6 ⚗️⚗️ A cup is stationary on a table.

Explain how the table provides a force that supports the cup. *(3 marks)*

_____

_____

_____

_____

7 ⚗️⚗️ **Figure 1** shows the same gas at different temperatures.

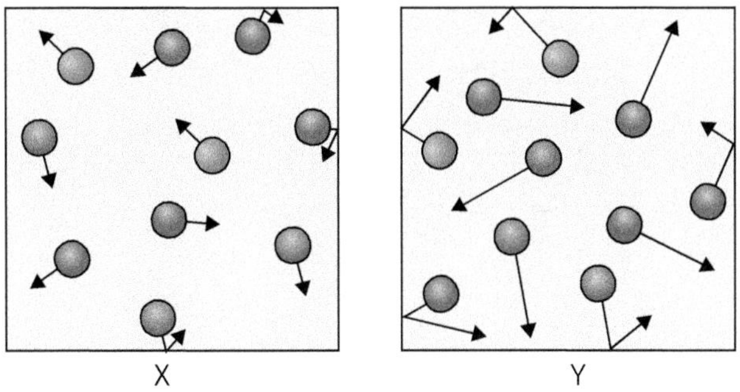

X   Y

Figure 1

a i Which of these images shows a hot gas and which shows a cold gas? *(1 mark)*

Hot gas _____

Cold gas _____

ii Decide which of these images shows the gas at a higher pressure. _____ *(1 mark)*

b i In a room at room temperature, 23 °C, two balloons are refilled with air. One is filled with air at 23 °C and the other air at 80 °C.

Explain why the balloon filled with hot air will rise, whereas the balloon filled with colder air will not. *(2 marks)*

_____

_____

_____

ii Draw a forces diagram for a balloon that is rising. *(1 mark)*

8 🧪🧪🧪 **a** Male stag beetles have jaws 30 mm long and a strong bite of 8.0 N.

Calculate the moment of force and include the units. Work in metres. The formula for moment of force is:

moment = force × distance from pivot   (*2 marks*)

_____

b Scissors are a type of lever.

When using scissors, it is easier to cut when the object is nearer to the pivot rather than at the end of the blade.

pivot

Figure 2

Explain why, using the concept of moments.

(*4 marks*)

_____

_____

_____

_____

_____

_____

9 🧪🧪🧪 A car is parked on a bridge. Describe what happens to the particles and bonds in the bridge to allow the bridge to support the car.   (*3 marks*)

_____

_____

_____

_____

10 🧪🧪🧪 A scientist investigates a new material and finds that it obeys Hooke's Law.

a When she applies a force of 1500 N, she observes that it stretches by 1.2 mm. Predict the extension for a force of 1 N (called the spring constant).

(*2 marks*)

_____

b **Table 2** shows readings that the scientist measured for a similar material. On the axes provided, plot the data and draw a line of best fit.   (*3 marks*)

Table 2

Force (N)	Extension (mm)
0	0.0
200	0.9
400	1.7
600	2.6
800	3.3
1000	4.0
1200	4.8
1400	5.6
1600	6.6

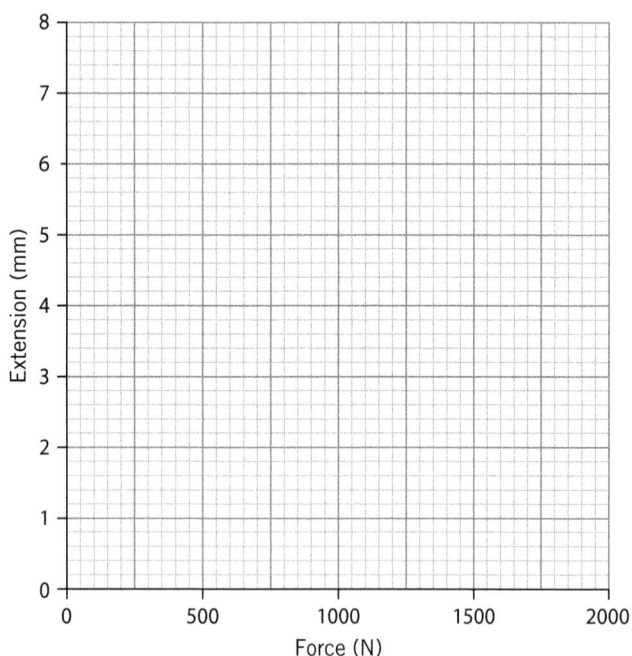

c Describe the relationship between the variables shown in your graph for part **b**.   (*1 mark*)

_____

_____

11 🧪🧪🧪 Finn is investigating electromagnets. For each change he makes to an electromagnet, circle the effect it will have on the electromagnet's strength and give a reason.

a An increase in current makes the strength **decrease / stay the same / increase** because

(*2 marks*)

_____

b A decrease in the number of turns on the coil makes the strength **decrease / stay the same / increase** because *(2 marks)*

_____

12 ⚗️⚗️⚗️ Explain whether each of the following materials is a thermal insulator or conductor and why.

a Copper *(2 marks)*

_____

_____

b Expanded polystyrene *(2 marks)*

_____

_____

13 ⚗️⚗️⚗️ Leah is a biologist working with animals that live very deep in the ocean. She has heard that animals can be harmed when they are brought up to the surface.

For each hypothesis below, give whether each cause is correct or not and a reason for your answer. *(6 marks)*

a "Water in animal's body expanding" is **correct / incorrect** because *(2 marks)*

_____

_____

b "Large increase in pressure" is **correct / incorrect** because *(2 marks)*

_____

_____

c "Large decrease in pressure" is **correct / incorrect** because *(2 marks)*

_____

_____

14 ⚗️⚗️⚗️ In a hospital, a radiographer is the person who carries out X-ray scans and so is exposed to ionising radiation. While they conduct a scan, the radiographer will wear a lead apron and move away from the scanner.

Explain in detail what ionising radiation is and how it causes harm. Why are similar precautions not needed for the microwaves used in a mobile phone or oven? *(6 marks)*

_____

_____

_____

_____

_____

_____

_____

_____

15 ⚗️⚗️⚗️ On a hot day, a child's ice cream will start to melt.

a Explain why this happens. What will the final temperature of the ice cream be? *(2 marks)*

_____

_____

_____

b Use each of the following keywords at least once to explain how energy is transferred between the ice cream and the air around it. *(4 marks)*

temperature	vibrating / moving	thermal
energy	transferred	particles	collide

_____

_____

_____

_____

_____

_____

c Why does an ice cream cone wrapped in shiny paper stay cold for longer? *(2 marks)*

_____

_____

_____

_____

Section 1 Checklist

Revision question number	Outcome	Topic reference	🙁	😐	🙂
1	Calculate work done.	3.3.1			
2a	Explain why fluids exert a pressure.	1.4.1			
2b, c	Calculate fluid pressure.	1.4.1			
3a	Compare transverse and longitudinal waves.	4.4.1			
3b	Draw an appropriate graph with a line of best fit.	EP7			
4	Describe different ways to insulate in terms of conduction, convection and radiation.	3.4.3			
5a	Describe how the magnetic field strength due to a current carrying wire varies with distance from the wire.	2.4.1			
5b	Describe how an electric bell, circuit breaker, or loudspeaker works.	2.4.2			
6	Explain how solid surfaces provide a support force.	1.3.2			
7a	Describe what happens when you heat up solids, liquids, and gases.	3.4.1			
7b	Explain why some things float and some things sink, using force diagrams.	1.4.2			
8a	Calculate the moment of a force.	1.3.3			
8b	Apply the concept of moments to everyday situations.	1.3.3			
9	Explain how solid surfaces provide a support force, using scientific terminology and bonding.	1.3.2			
10a	Apply Hooke's Law to make quantitative predictions with unfamiliar materials.	1.3.2			
10b, c	Present data in a graph and recognise quantitative patterns and errors.	1.3.2			
11	Predict the effect of changes made to an electromagnet, using scientific knowledge to justify the claim.	2.4.1			
12	Explain why certain materials are good thermal insulators.	3.4.2			
13	Explain why liquid pressure changes with depth.	1.4.2			
14	Explain why only some electromagnetic waves cause ionisation. Explain why ionisation can be harmful to living cells.	4.3.2			
15a	Describe how energy is transferred through solids, liquids, and in air.	3.4.1			
15b	Explain, in terms of particles, how energy is transferred.	3.4.1			
15c	Explain why certain materials are good thermal insulators.	3.4.2			

5.3.1 Elements

A Fill in the gaps to complete the sentences.

An element is a substance that cannot be broken down into other _____. There are 98 naturally

occurring _____, and they are all listed in the _____ Table. Every element has its own

_____ symbol, which is a one- or two-letter code for the element. Scientists all over the world use

the same chemical _____ for the elements.

B **a** Tick the **four** true statements below.

    1 Every material, and everything in the Universe, is made up of one or more elements. ☐

    2 It is possible to break down an element into other substances. ☐

    3 There are about 1000 naturally occurring elements. ☐

    4 A chemical symbol is the one- or two-letter code for an element. ☐

    5 Scientists in the UK and China use the same symbol for the element bromine. ☐

    6 The chemical symbol of sodium in So. ☐

    7 The chemical symbol of bromine is br. ☐

    8 The chemical symbol of iron is Fe. ☐

  b Write corrected versions of the **four** statements that are not true.

_____

_____

_____

_____

C Complete the table.

Name of element	Chemical symbol
	H
carbon	
	N
oxygen	
	Na
magnesium	
	Al
sulfur	

Name of element	Chemical symbol
	Cl
potassium	
	Fe
copper	
	Zn
bromine	
	I
tungsten	

Hint: The first letter of a chemical symbol is upper case, and the second letter is lower case.

D Suggest **one** advantage of using the same chemical symbols in all languages.

_____

5.3.2 Atoms

A Fill in the gaps to complete the sentences.

Elements are made up of _____ . An atom is the _____ part of an element that can

exist. All the _____ of an element are the same. The atoms of one element are _____

from the atoms of all the other elements. The properties of an element are the properties of _____

atoms joined together.

B The statements below are about two elements, copper and zinc.

   a Tick the statements that are true.

      1 An element is the smallest part of an atom that can exist. ☐

      2 The atoms of copper are all the same as each other. ☐

      3 The atoms of copper are the same as the atoms of zinc. ☐

      4 A single atom of zinc has the same properties as a piece of zinc wire. ☐

      5 A copper wire can conduct electricity, but a single copper atom cannot conduct electricity. ☐

   b Now write corrected versions of the **three** statements above that are not true.

_____

_____

_____

C A piece of solid copper melts.

   a Describe the changes in the arrangement and movement of its atoms.

_____

_____

   b Explain why one copper atom on its own cannot melt.

_____

_____

D In 12 g of carbon there are approximately 600 000 million million million atoms.

   a Estimate the number of atoms in 6 g of carbon.

                                             _____

   b Estimate the number of atoms in 24 g of carbon.

                                             _____

   c Estimate the mass of carbon that contains 60 000 million million million atoms.

                                             _____

5.3.3 Compounds

A Fill in the gaps to complete the sentences.

A compound is a substance that is made up of atoms of two or more _____. The atoms are

_____ joined together. The properties of a compound are _____ from the properties

of the elements whose atoms are in it because the atoms are joined together to make _____

substance. A molecule is a group of _____ that are joined together _____.

Molecules can contain more than one _____ of the same element, for example hydrogen,

or _____ of two or more different elements..

B The diagrams show molecules of elements and compounds.

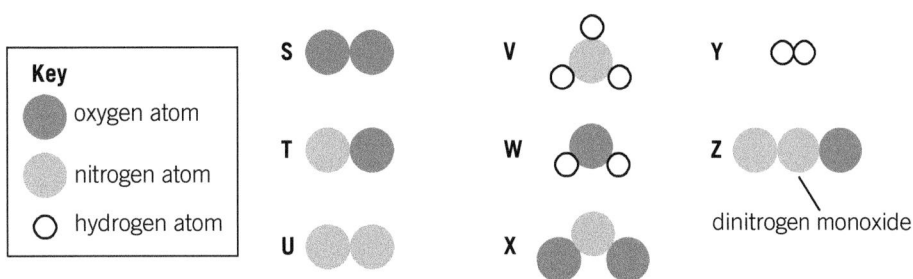

a Draw circles around the molecules of compounds.

b Explain why the diagrams you circled are compounds.

_____

C Nitrogen and oxygen are gases in the air. They are elements.
Oxygen helps substances to burn. Crisp bags are filled with nitrogen to stop the crisps going stale.
Dinitrogen monoxide is a compound. It is used to relieve pain in childbirth.

Choose molecule diagrams from activity **B** to help you to answer the questions below.

a Write down the number of atoms in one nitrogen molecule. _____

b Write down the number of atoms in one dinitrogen monoxide molecule. _____

c Write down the number of elements whose atoms are in one nitrogen molecule. _____

d Write down the number of elements whose atoms are in one dinitrogen monoxide molecule. _____

D The table shows the properties of three substances.

Substance	Melting point (°C)	Appearance	Is it attracted to a magnet?
iron	1535	shiny and grey	yes
sulfur	113	yellow	no
iron sulfide	1194	shiny and grey	no

a Describe **one** way in which iron sulfide is similar to the elements it is made from.

_____

b Describe **two** ways in which iron sulfide is different from the elements it is made from.

_____

c Suggest why most of the properties of iron sulfide are different from the properties of the elements it is
made from.

_____

3.4 Chemical formulae

A Fill in the gaps to complete the sentences.

A _____ formula uses chemical symbols to show the elements in a substance. It also shows the

number of atoms of one element compared to the _____ of atoms of another element. For example,

the chemical formula of water is H_2O. This shows that water is made up of two elements – hydrogen and

_____. It also shows that there are two atoms of hydrogen for every _____ atom of oxygen.

B Complete the table.

Name of compound	Atoms in compound	Formula of compound
magnesium oxide	one atom of magnesium for every one atom of oxygen	
calcium chloride		$CaCl_2$
	one atom of nitrogen for every two atoms of oxygen	NO_2
carbon monoxide		
		SO_3

C Complete the sentences below by writing one **number** in each gap.

Sulfur dioxide, SO_2, has _____ oxygen atoms for every one sulfur atom. The total number of atoms in one sulfur

dioxide molecule is _____.

Methane, CH_4, is a gas used for cooking. It has _____ hydrogen atoms for every one carbon atom. The total number

of atoms in one methane molecule is _____.

Ethanol, C_2H_6O, is the compound in alcoholic drinks. Its molecules have atoms of _____ different elements. It has

_____ hydrogen atoms for every one carbon atom.

D The table shows the relative masses of atoms of three elements.

Element	Relative mass of atoms
hydrogen	1
carbon	12
oxygen	16

Calculate the relative formula mass of the elements and compounds below. Show your working.

a Oxygen, O_2

_____

b Water, H_2O

_____

c Ibuprofen, $C_{13}H_{18}O_2$

_____

d Name the element in ibuprofen whose atoms contribute the greatest mass to the compound.

_____

Hint: Start by calculating the total mass of the carbon atoms shown in the formula. Repeat for the hydrogen and oxygen atoms.

5.3.5 Polymers

A Fill in the gaps to complete the sentences.

A polymer is a substance with very _____ molecules. Its molecules have identical groups of atoms,

repeated _____ times. There are _____ polymers, each with _____

properties. The properties of polymers depend on the groups of _____ in their molecules.

B The table shows data for some polymers.

Polymer	Strength when pulled (MPa)	Density (g/cm³)	Flexibility	Is it waterproof?
LDPE	15	0.92	very flexible	yes
HDPE	15	0.96	rigid	yes
Poly(propene)	40	0.90	very flexible	yes
flexible PVC	20	1.30	very flexible	yes
rigid PVC	60	1.30	rigid	yes
nylon 6	70	1.13	very flexible	yes

a Poly(propene) is used to make ropes for ships. Use data from the table to explain why it is suitable for this use.

_____

b Catherine says that it would be better to make ropes from nylon 6 than from poly(propene). Choose data from the table to suggest why.

_____

c Choose two polymers that are suitable for making water bottles. Give reasons for your choices.

Polymers: _____ and _____

Reasons: _____

d Compare the properties of LDPE and flexible PVC.

_____

_____

_____

Hint: Write about how the two polymers are similar, and how they are different. Include data from the table in your answer.

C The diagrams show the molecules in two different polymers.

Suggest why polymer **X** is flexible and polymer **Y** is rigid.

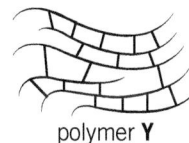

polymer **X**   polymer **Y**

_____

_____

_____

D Outdoor chairs can be made of wood or synthetic polymers such as high-density poly(ethene), HDPE. Use information from the table, and your own knowledge, to compare the advantages and disadvantages of the two materials.

_____

_____

_____

_____

5.4.1 The Periodic Table

A Fill in the gaps to complete the sentences.

In the Periodic Table, the vertical columns are called _____ and the horizontal rows are called

_____. There are patterns in the properties of the elements down _____ and across

_____. You can use patterns in the melting point of the elements in a _____ to predict

the melting point of an element whose melting point you do not know.

B The tables show the densities of some Group 3 and Group 4 elements.
Boron is at the top of Group 3 of the Periodic Table, and carbon is at the top of Group 4.

Group 3 element	Density (g/cm³)
boron	2.3
aluminium	2.7
gallium	5.9
indium	7.3
thallium	11.8

Group 4 element	Density (g/cm³)
carbon	2.2
silicon	2.3
germanium	5.3
tin	7.3
lead	

a A piece of lead has a volume of 5.0 cm³ and a mass of 56.5 g.

Calculate the density of lead. **Hint:** Use the equation: $\text{density} = \dfrac{\text{mass}}{\text{volume}}$

_____ g/cm³

b Compare the patterns in density for Group 3 and Group 4.

_____

_____

Hint: Describe the pattern in Group 3, then describe the pattern in Group 4. Then identify whether the patterns are similar or different.

C The tables below show data for elements in neighbouring groups in the Periodic Table.
Each table shows the elements in one group.

The groups are arranged in the same order in the Periodic Table.

Period	Element	Melting point (°C)	Element	Melting point (°C)	Element	Melting point (°C)	Element	Melting point (°C)
4	Ti	1675	V	1900	Cr	1890	Mn	1240
5	Zr	1850	Nb	2470	Mo	2610	Tc	2200
6	Hf		Ta	3000	W	3410	Re	3180

a Compare the patterns in melting point for the Period 4 and Period 5 elements.

_____

_____

_____

b Suggest a value for the melting point of hafnium, Hf, and explain your prediction.

Melting point _____ °C

Reason _____

5.4.2 The elements of Group 1

A Fill in the gaps to complete the sentences.

Group 1 contains the elements in the column on the _____ of the Periodic Table. The Group 1

elements are metals. They _____ electricity and have _____ densities. The Group 1

elements react vigorously with water – in other words, they are very _____. When a Group 1 element

reacts with water, _____ substances are made. These substances are _____ gas and a

metal _____.

B The bar chart shows the melting and boiling points of the Group 1 elements.

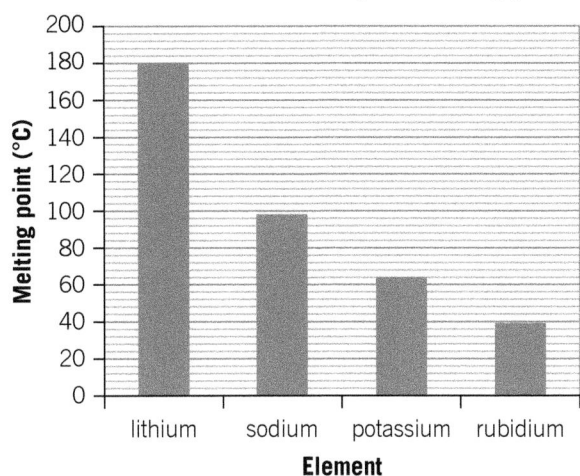

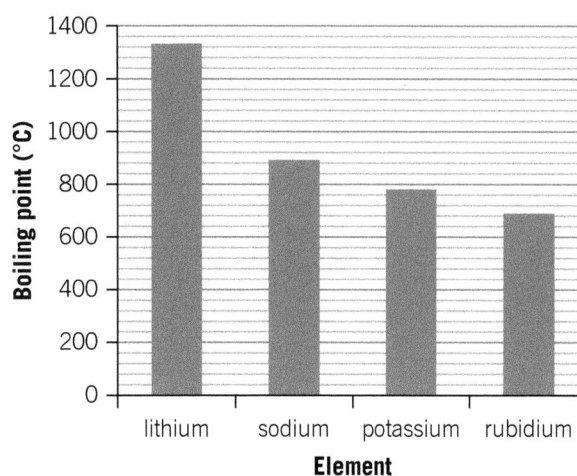

a Describe the trend in boiling point for the Group 1 elements.

_____

_____

b Compare the patterns in melting point and boiling point for the Group 1 elements.

_____

_____

Hint: Look at the scales on the *y*-axis – they are different.

c Predict the melting point of caesium, which is below rubidium in Group 1.

_____ °C

C Dr Naylor heated three Group 1 elements in chlorine gas. The table shows what his students observed.

Group 1 element	Appearance during heating in chlorine gas	Appearance of product
lithium	burns well with red flame	white solid
sodium	burns strongly with bright orange flame	white solid
potassium	burns very strongly with lilac flame	white solid

a Describe **two** similarities between the reaction of chlorine with each of the Group 1 elements shown in the table.

_____

b Predict the appearance of the product formed when rubidium is heated in chlorine gas.

_____

c Predict the name of the product formed when caesium is heated in chlorine gas.

_____

5.4.3 The elements of Group 7

A Fill in the gaps to complete the sentences.

Group 7 contains the elements in the column that is second from the _____ of the Periodic Table.

The elements in Group 7 are also called the _____. They are non-_____. The Group 7

elements take part in displacement _____.

B A bottle of bromine has two hazard symbols.
Draw a line to match each hazard symbol to its meaning and risk. Then complete the empty boxes by writing one way of controlling each risk.

Hazard symbol	Meaning	Risk from this hazard	How to control the risk
	corrosive	difficulty breathing	
	toxic	burns eyes	

C A student mixes the solutions shown in the table. She does **not** mix the solutions shown by the shaded boxes.
The observations she makes are given in the list **V** to **Z** below.

Observations

V pale green and colourless solutions react to make an orange solution ☐

W orange and colourless solutions react to make a brown solution ☐

X pale green and colourless solutions react to make a brown solution ☐

Y no change observed ☐

Z orange and colourless solutions react to make a green solution ☐

Complete the table by writing the letters of the correct observations for each reaction. You can use each letter once, more than once, or not at all.

	Potassium chloride solution	Potassium bromide solution	Potassium iodide solution
chlorine solution			
bromine solution			
iodine solution			

Hint: There is a displacement reaction when a more reactive element is mixed with a solution of a salt of a less reactive element. The Group 7 elements get **less** reactive from top to bottom of the group.

D a A student adds a halogen solution to sodium bromide solution. She observes a definite colour change. Predict the position of the halogen in the Periodic Table, compared to the position of bromine.

_____

b Justify your prediction in part **a**.

_____

_____

5.4.4 The elements of Group 0

A Fill in the gaps to complete the sentences.

Group 0 contains the elements in the column on the _____ of the Periodic Table. The elements in

Group 0 are also called the _____ gases. They are non-_____. Most Group 0 elements

do not take part in chemical reactions – in other words, they are _____.

B a Draw one line from each element to show its chemical reactions.

Element

| **a** helium |
| **b** neon |
| **c** krypton |
| **d** xenon |

Chemical reactions

| **1** reacts with fluorine, the most reactive element |
| **2** reacts with oxygen and fluorine, which are very reactive |
| **3** none |

b Write a conclusion about the reactivity of the Group 0 elements and how this changes down the group.

_____

_____

C The table shows melting point data for the Group 0 elements.

a Describe the pattern in melting point for Group 0.

_____

b Predict the melting point of krypton, and explain how you made your prediction.

_____

_____

Element	Melting point (°C)
helium	−270
neon	−249
argon	−189
krypton	
xenon	−112

D The bar charts show the boiling points of the Group 1 and Group 0 elements.

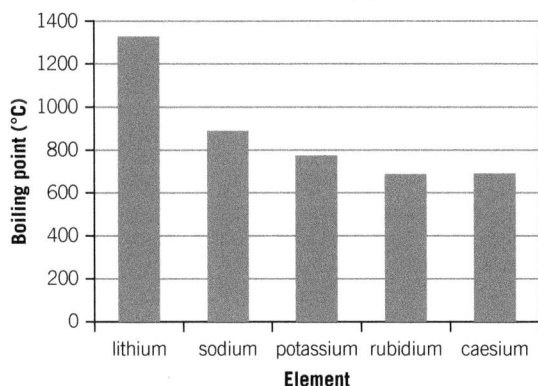

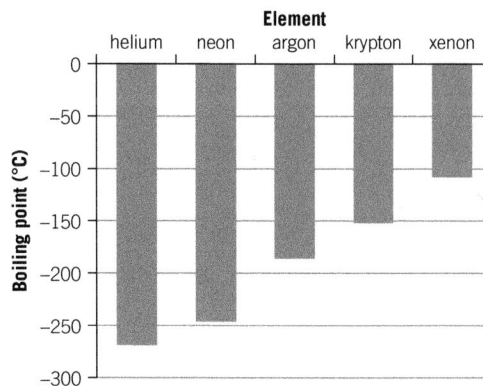

Compare the patterns in boiling points for the Group 1 and Group 0 elements.

_____

_____

Big Idea 5 Pinchpoint ⊗

Pinchpoint question

Answer the question below, then do the follow-up activity **with the same letter** as the answer you picked.

This question is about the displacement reactions of the Group 7 elements. Which option below shows a displacement reaction that occurs **with** a correct explanation? You will need to use the Periodic Table in the back of this book.

A bromine + potassium fluoride → potassium bromide + fluorine
The reaction occurs because all Group 7 elements are very reactive.

B bromine + potassium iodide → potassium bromide + iodine
The reaction occurs because bromine is more reactive than iodine.

C bromine + potassium chloride → potassium bromide + chlorine
The reaction occurs because chlorine is more reactive than bromine.

D chlorine + potassium fluoride → potassium chloride + fluorine
The reaction occurs because chlorine is more reactive than the other elements in Group 7.

Follow-up activities

A In a displacement reaction, a more reactive Group 7 element pushes out a less reactive Group 7 element from its compound.

   a In each pair of elements below, underline the name of the **more** reactive Group 7 element.

      iodine and bromine

      chlorine and iodine

      fluorine and chlorine

      bromine and chlorine

      Hint: Start by listing the Group 7 elements in order of reactivity, most reactive first.

   b i Look at the pairs of substances below. Underline the pairs where a displacement reaction will occur.

      iodine and potassium bromide

      bromine and potassium iodide

      fluorine and potassium chloride

      chlorine and potassium fluoride

      chlorine and potassium iodide

      bromine and potassium chloride

   ii Write a word equation for each of the pairs that you underlined in part **i**.

      _____

      _____

      _____

      Hint: A displacement reaction occurs between a pair of substances if the **more** reactive Group 7 element is on its own, and if the **less** reactive Group 7 element is part of a compound. For help, see 5.4.3 The elements of Group 7.

B a Highlight or underline the **three** pairs of substances that react together in displacement reactions.

fluorine and potassium chloride

chlorine and potassium iodide

iodine and potassium fluoride

fluorine and potassium bromide

iodine and potassium bromide

bromine and potassium fluoride

b Write a word equation for each of the pairs that you underlined in part **a**.

_____

_____

_____

Hint: For help, see 5.4.3 The elements of Group 7.

C Some of the sentences below include one or more mistakes.
Read the sentences and correct the mistakes.

A displacement reaction occurs between a pair of substances if the less reactive Group 7 element is on its own, and if the more reactive Group 7 element is part of a compound.

Fluorine is more reactive than chlorine. This means that fluorine and potassium chloride do not react together in a displacement reaction.

Iodine is more reactive than bromine. This means that potassium iodide and bromine react together in a decomposition reaction. The products are iodine and potassium bromine.

Hint: In a displacement reaction, a **more** reactive Group 7 element pushes out a **less** reactive Group 7 element from its compound. For help, see 5.4.3 The elements of Group 7.

D a List the first four elements in Group 7, from most reactive to least reactive.

_____

_____

_____

_____

b Tick the true statements below.

1 Fluorine is more reactive than chlorine. ☐
2 There is no reaction between fluorine and potassium chloride. ☐
3 Iodine is more reactive than bromine. ☐
4 There is a displacement reaction between potassium iodide and bromine. ☐
5 Chlorine is less reactive than iodine. ☐
6 There is no reaction between potassium chloride and iodine. ☐
7 Fluorine is the least reactive element in Group 7. ☐
8 Fluorine displaces all the other Group 7 elements from their compounds with sodium. ☐

c Write corrected versions of the **four** statements that are not true.

_____

_____

_____

_____

_____

_____

_____

_____

Hint: A displacement reaction occurs when a **more** reactive Group 7 element on its own displaces, or pushes out, a **less** reactive Group 7 element from its compound. For help, see 5.4.3 The elements of Group 7.

Pinchpoint review

Now look back at the question – do you think you chose the right letter?
Turn to the Answers page to find out.

6.3.1 Atoms in chemical reactions

A Fill in the gaps to complete the sentences.

In a chemical reaction, the starting substances are the _____, and the substances that are made are

the _____. Word equations represent chemical reactions. In a word equation, the reactants are on

the _____ of the arrow and the products are on the _____. In a chemical reaction,

_____ are rearranged. The atoms are joined together _____ before and after the

reaction. There are the same number of atoms of each element before and _____ the reaction;

in other words, atoms are conserved.

B Complete the word equations for the reactions described below.

    a Sulfur burns in oxygen to make sulfur dioxide.

        sulfur + _____ → sulfur dioxide

    b Sodium reacts with chlorine to make sodium chloride.

        sodium + _____ → sodium _____

    c Methane burns in oxygen to make carbon dioxide and water.

        methane + _____ → _____ _____ + _____

C The particle diagram represents the reaction of methane with oxygen. It shows the atoms before and after the reaction.

    a Name the two reactants: _____ and _____

    b Name the two products: _____ and _____

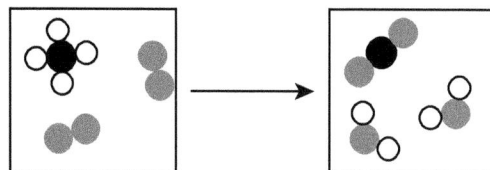

Key
● carbon atom ○ hydrogen atom ● oxygen atom

    c Using the information in the diagram, complete the table below.

Type of atom	Number of atoms of this type in reactants	Number of atoms of this type in products
carbon		
hydrogen		
oxygen		

    d Explain what happens to the atoms in any chemical reaction.

    _____

D The particle diagram below represents the reaction of carbon with oxygen.

Explain in detail what the particle diagram shows.

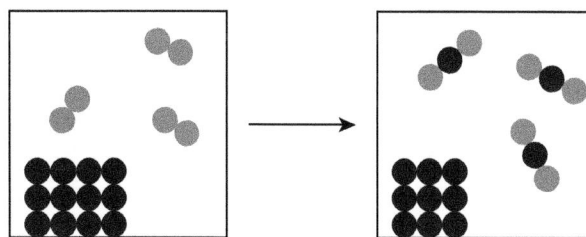

Key ● oxygen atom ● carbon atom

_____

_____

_____

_____

Hint: Has all the carbon reacted?

6.3.2 Burning fuels

A Fill in the gaps to complete the sentences.

A fuel is a material that burns to transfer _____ by heating. The scientific word for burning

is _____. When a fuel burns it reacts with _____ from the air. The product of

combustion of carbon is _____ _____. The products of combustion of a compound

that is made from carbon and hydrogen atoms are carbon dioxide and _____. Burning reactions are

oxidation reactions. In oxidation reactions, substances react with _____. Petrol, diesel, and coal are

fossil _____. They cannot be replaced once they have been used, so they are called

_____-_____ fuels.

B The products of a combustion reaction are the substances that are made when a substance burns.

a Complete the table with the names of the products of combustion.
Then complete the balanced symbol equations by writing in the missing formulae and balancing numbers.

Fuel	Product or products of combustion	Word equation for combustion reaction
charcoal (a form of carbon)		carbon + oxygen → _____ _____
hydrogen		hydrogen + _____ → water
heptane (a compound of carbon and hydrogen that is in petrol)		heptane + _____ → _____ _____ + water

b Explain why burning hydrogen is better for the environment than burning heptane.

_____

_____

C Riley does an investigation to compare the increase in temperature of water when two different fuels burn. Here is a diagram of the apparatus. The fuels are wax and ethanol.

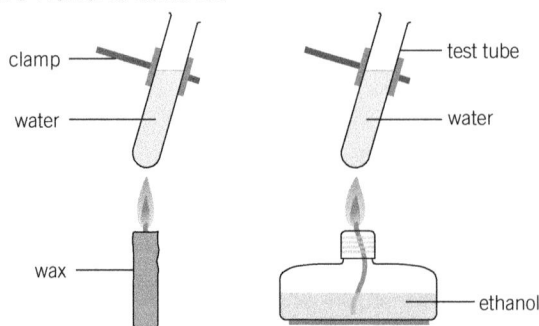

a Draw a line to match each variable to the type of variable it is in this investigation.

volume of water

increase in temperature of water

fuel

distance of flame from test tube

independent

dependent

control

b Suggest **one** improvement that Riley could make to maximise the amount of energy transferred from the fuel to the water.

_____

6.3.3 Thermal decomposition

A Fill in the gaps to complete the sentences.

In a decomposition reaction, _____ reactant breaks down to make _____ or more

products. The reactant must be a _____. The products can be elements or _____.

Zinc carbonate, for example, decomposes to make zinc _____ and _____

_____. When heat is needed to make a substance break down, the reaction is called a

_____ decomposition reaction.

B **a** Highlight or underline the word equation that shows a decomposition reaction.

    X   methane + oxygen → carbon dioxide + water

    Y   sodium nitrate → sodium nitrite + oxygen

  b Explain why the reaction you chose in part **a** is a decomposition reaction.

_____

C The word equations below show four thermal decomposition reactions:

    copper carbonate → copper oxide + carbon dioxide

    zinc carbonate → zinc oxide + carbon dioxide

    calcium nitrate → calcium oxide + nitrogen dioxide + oxygen

    magnesium nitrate → magnesium oxide + nitrogen dioxide + oxygen

  a Lead carbonate decomposes to make lead oxide and carbon dioxide. Write a word equation for the reaction.

_____

  b Devise a general rule to describe the products formed when a metal carbonate decomposes on heating.

_____

  c Predict the names of the products of the thermal decomposition reaction of strontium nitrate.

_____

D Raj heats copper carbonate in the apparatus shown in the diagram.

He writes the time for the limewater to go milky in the table below.

He then repeats the experiment with two more compounds.

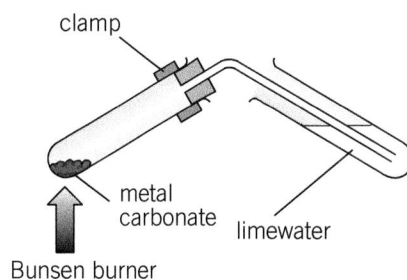

clamp

metal carbonate

limewater

Bunsen burner

Compound	Time for limewater to start looking cloudy (minutes)
copper carbonate	1
potassium carbonate	did not go cloudy after heating for 10 minutes
lead carbonate	4

Write a conclusion for Raj's investigation.

In your conclusion, name the carbonate that decomposes most easily.

_____

_____

_____

6.3.4 Conservation of mass

A Fill in the gaps to complete the sentences.

In a chemical reaction or in a _____ change, the total mass does not change because the total

number of atoms is the _____ in the reactants and products. This means that in a chemical reaction,

the total mass of reactants is equal to the total mass of _____ . This is the law of _____

of mass. Balanced symbol equations show the relative amounts of _____ and products.

B Hydrogen and oxygen react together to make water: hydrogen + oxygen → water

The diagrams show some of the atoms before and after the reaction.

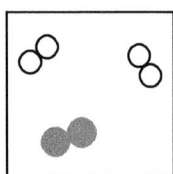

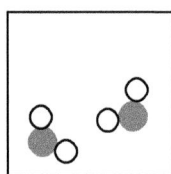

Before the reaction   After the reaction

Key
○ hydrogen atom
● oxygen atom

   a Use the diagrams to explain why the total mass of hydrogen and oxygen that reacts is the same as the mass of water made.

_____

   b Use the diagrams above to help you to balance the chemical equation below.

_____ H_2 + O_2 → _____ H_2O

Hint: You need to write one number on each line.

C Calculate the missing masses in the reactions below.

   a   carbon   +   oxygen   →   carbon dioxide
                 12 g   32 g   _____ g

   b   calcium carbonate   →   calcium oxide   +   carbon dioxide
                10 g   5.6 g   _____ g

   c   calcium nitrate   →   calcium oxide   +   nitrogen dioxide   +   oxygen
              32.8 g   _____ g   18.4 g   3.2 g

D A teacher demonstrates three reactions.

Tick one column next to each reaction to show whether the mass of the substances in the reaction vessel increases, decreases, or does not change.

	Reaction	✓ if mass increases	✓ if mass decreases	✓ if mass does not change
a	Solid lead nitrate reacts with solid potassium iodide to make solid lead iodide and solid potassium nitrate.			
b	Solid magnesium reacts with oxygen gas from the air to make solid magnesium oxide.			
c	Solid copper carbonate decomposes to make solid copper oxide and carbon dioxide gas.			
d	aluminium (solid) + iodine (solid) → aluminium iodide (solid)			

   e Explain your answers to parts **b** and **d**.

_____

_____

_____

6.4.1 Exothermic and endothermic

A Fill in the gaps to complete the sentences.

Chemical reactions and physical changes involve _____ transfers. Exothermic reactions transfer

energy _____ the reaction mixture _____ the surroundings. This causes the

temperature of the surroundings to _____.

Endothermic reactions transfer energy _____ the surroundings _____ the reaction

mixture. This causes the temperature of the surroundings to _____.

Physical changes, including dissolving and changes of state, also involve _____ transfers. In an

_____ change, energy is transferred to the surroundings. In an _____ change, energy

is transferred from the surroundings.

B Barney sets up the apparatus shown.

He pours dilute hydrochloric acid into the cup, and measures its temperature.

Then he adds a piece of magnesium ribbon. There is a chemical reaction.

At the end of the chemical reaction he measures the temperature again.

Then Barney repeats the experiment with zinc instead of magnesium.

Some of his results are in the table.

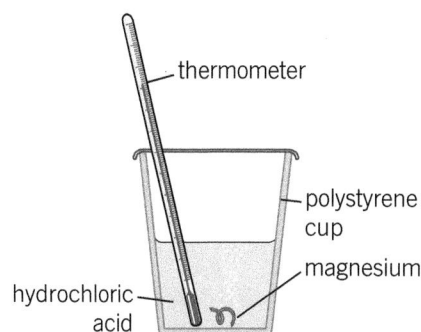

Reacting substances	Temperature before the reaction (°C)	Temperature after the reaction (°C)	Temperature change (°C)
hydrochloric acid and magnesium	20	78	
hydrochloric acid and zinc	20	28	

a Complete the table by filling in the missing values.

b Write a conclusion for Barney's experiment.

_____

_____

_____

_____

Hint: In your conclusion, state whether the reactions are exothermic or endothermic.

C Sarah investigates the temperature changes when different substances dissolve in water. First, she uses a data book to find out whether each substance dissolves exothermically or endothermically.

Substance	Does it dissolve exothermically or endothermically?
aluminium chloride	exothermically
sodium chloride	endothermically
magnesium chloride	exothermically
potassium chloride	endothermically

a Predict the **two** substances in the table that make the temperature of the water increase at first when they dissolve in water.

_____ and _____

b Choose **two** substances from the table that could be used in a hand warmer. Justify your choice.

_____

_____

6.4.2 Energy level diagrams

A Fill in the gaps to complete the sentences.

An energy level diagram for a chemical reaction shows the relative amounts of energy stored in the reactants

and _____. An energy level diagram for a physical change shows the relative amounts of energy

in the substance before and _____ the change. In an energy level diagram, if the horizontal line

on the left is higher, the reaction is _____. If the horizontal line on the left is lower, the reaction is

_____.

B The energy level diagram below represents the energy change when liquid oxygen boils.

Tick the statements that are **true** for the change shown in the diagram.

1   Liquid oxygen stores more energy than the same amount of oxygen gas.   ☐

2   The substance at the start stores less energy than the substance at the end.   ☐

3   During the change, energy is transferred from the surroundings to the
boiling oxygen.   ☐

4   The change is exothermic.   ☐

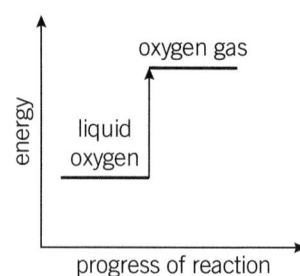

C The table shows the energy transferred to the surroundings when three different
fuels burn.

Fuel	Energy stored by fuel (kJ/g)
ethanol	27
hydrogen	120
petrol	44

Write **three** sentences to compare the amounts of energy transferred when 1 g of each of the fuels in the table burns.

_____

_____

_____

Hint: Approximately how many times as much energy is transferred by burning 1 g of hydrogen compared to burning 1 g of petrol?

D The energy level diagram shows the energy change that occurs
when substance X dissolves in water.

a   Add labels to the two horizontal lines.

b   Explain what the arrow shows.

_____

_____

c   Explain whether the process of dissolving substance X in water
would be more suitable for heating food, or keeping it cool.

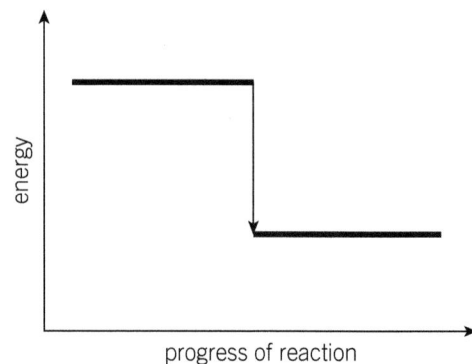

_____

_____

Hint: In this question, 'explain' means that you must write down your choice and give a reason for it.

6.4.3 Bond energies

A Fill in the gaps to complete the sentences.

A chemical reaction starts when bonds between atoms in the reactants _____. This process requires

energy from the surroundings, so is _____. Then new bonds form between atoms to make the

_____. This process transfers energy to the surroundings, so is _____.

Overall, a chemical reaction is endothermic if the energy required to break bonds is _____ than

the energy released in making new bonds. A reaction is exothermic if the energy required to break bonds is

_____ than the energy released in making new bonds. A substance that speeds up a chemical

reaction without being changed itself is a _____.

B The energy level diagram below represents the chemical reaction
of nitrogen with oxygen to make nitrogen monoxide:

nitrogen + oxygen → nitrogen monoxide

a In the table below, write a label for each arrow shown on the diagram.

Arrow	Label
X	
Y	
Z	

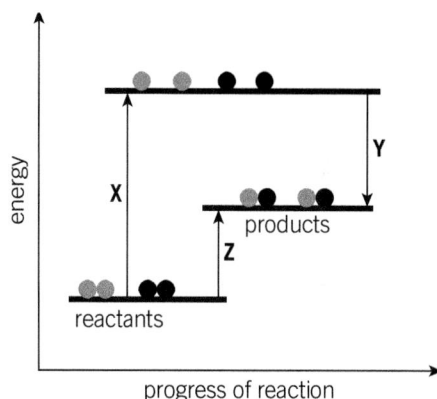

b Use the energy level diagram above to explain why the reaction shown in the word equation is endothermic.

_____

_____

_____

Hint: In your answer, compare the energy required to break bonds in the reactants to the energy released when
new bonds are made in the products.

C Hydrogen reacts with chlorine to make hydrogen chloride:

$H_2(g) + Cl_2(g) \rightarrow 2HCl(g)$

The table shows the bond energies of the bonds that are involved
in the reaction.

Bond	Bond energy (kJ/mol)
H–H	436
Cl–Cl	243
H–Cl	432

a Choose data from the table to calculate the energy needed
to break the bonds in the reactants.

_____

b Choose data from the table to calculate the energy released when the bond in the product is made, for the
number of molecules shown in the chemical equation.

_____

c Explain whether the reaction is endothermic or exothermic.

_____

Pinchpoint question

Answer the question below, then do the follow-up activity **with the same letter** as the answer you picked.

A student heats copper carbonate in test tube **X**.

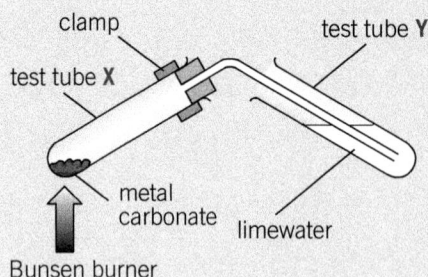

The copper carbonate decomposes to make copper oxide and carbon dioxide gas:

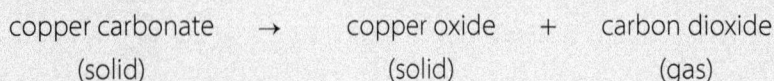

copper carbonate	→	copper oxide	+	carbon dioxide
(solid)		(solid)		(gas)

The gas bubbles into the limewater in test tube **Y**. Another chemical reaction takes place. The products are in the solid and liquid states.

Which statement correctly describes and explains any changes in mass in the contents of test tubes **X** and **Y**?

A The mass of **X** does not change because the product that leaves **X** is in the gas state.
The mass of **Y** does not change because the reactant that enters **Y** is in the gas state.

B The masses of **X** and **Y** do not change because, for the chemical reaction in each test tube, the total mass of products is equal to total mass of reactants.

C The masses of **X** and **Y** increase because new substances are made in each test tube.

D The mass of **X** decreases because a product in the gas state leaves the test tube.
The mass of **Y** increases because a reactant in the gas state enters the test tube.

Follow-up activities

A The diagrams show particles when a substance is in the solid state and when it is in the gas state.

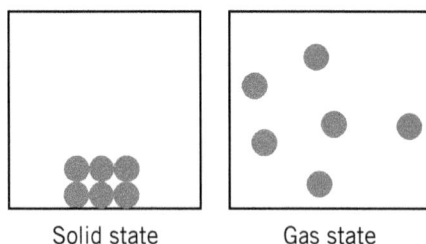

Solid state   Gas state

Tick the statements below that are true.

1 A particle has the same mass when the substance is in the solid and gas states. ☐
2 One thousand particles of a substance in the gas state have a smaller mass than one thousand particles of the same substance in the solid state. ☐
3 A particle has no mass when the substance is in the gas state. ☐
4 A gas has mass. ☐

Hint: Do the particles change when a substance changes state? For help, see 5.1.2 States of matter.

B A teacher demonstrates three reactions.

Draw a line to show, for each reaction, whether the total mass of solid substance(s) in the reaction vessel increases, decreases, or does not change. You can choose an option more than once.

Solid calcium carbonate decomposes to make solid calcium oxide and carbon dioxide gas.

Solid carbon reacts with oxygen from the air to make carbon dioxide gas.

mass decreases

Solid magnesium reacts with oxygen from the air to make solid magnesium oxide.

mass increases

Solid magnesium nitrate decomposes on heating to make solid magnesium oxide, nitrogen dioxide gas, and oxygen gas.

Solid zinc reacts with oxygen from the air to make solid zinc oxide.

mass does not change

Solid lead nitrate and solid potassium iodide react to make solid lead iodide and solid potassium nitrate.

Hint: How does the mass change if the reaction makes a gas, which escapes to the air? For help, see 6.3.4 Conservation of mass.

C The diagrams show some atoms before and after the chemical reaction of nitrogen and oxygen to make nitrogen monoxide.

Each sentence below has one mistake. Write a corrected version of each sentence.

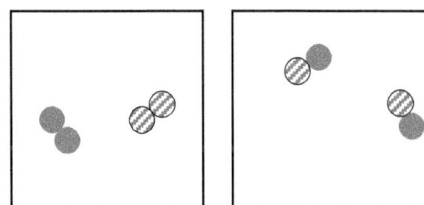

Reactants   Product

a The mass of a nitrogen atom in the product is greater than the mass of a nitrogen atom in the reactants.

_____

b The mass of an oxygen atom in the product is less than the mass of an oxygen atom in the reactants.

_____

c In the chemical reaction, the atoms are not rearranged.

_____

d In the chemical reaction, the atoms are joined together in the same way before and after the reaction.

_____

e There are more atoms in the products than in the reactants.

_____

f The total mass of products is greater than the total mass of reactants.

_____

Hint: Are new atoms made in chemical reactions? For help, see 6.3.4 Conservation of mass.

D Explain each observation below.

a On burning solid magnesium in air, the mass of solid product is greater than the mass of solid reactant.

_____

_____

b On heating lead carbonate to make it decompose, the mass of solid product is less than the mass of solid reactant.

_____

_____

c On reacting solid lead nitrate and solid potassium iodide, two products are formed in the solid state. The mass of solid product is the same as the mass of the solid reactant.

_____

_____

d On warming hydrogen peroxide solution, the products are water and oxygen gas. The mass of solution after heating is less than the mass of solution before heating.

_____

_____

Hint: What are the states of the reactants and products in each reaction? For help, see 6.3.4 Conservation of mass.

Pinchpoint review
Now look back at the question – do you think you chose the right letter?
Turn to the Answers page to find out.

7.3.1 Global warming

A Fill in the gaps to complete the sentences.

The air around us is called the _____. The greenhouse effect is when energy from the Sun is

_____ to the thermal energy store of gases in the Earth's atmosphere. Greenhouse gases include

methane and carbon _____. Global warming is the gradual increase in the air _____

at the surface of the Earth.

B The numbered statements below are labels for the diagram.

Write the number of one label next to each arrow on the
diagram, to show what the arrow represents.

1 The Earth's surface emits radiation.

2 The Sun warms the Earth's surface.

3 The atmosphere reflects and absorbs some radiation from
the Sun.

4 The atmosphere absorbs and radiates some radiation from
the Earth's surface.

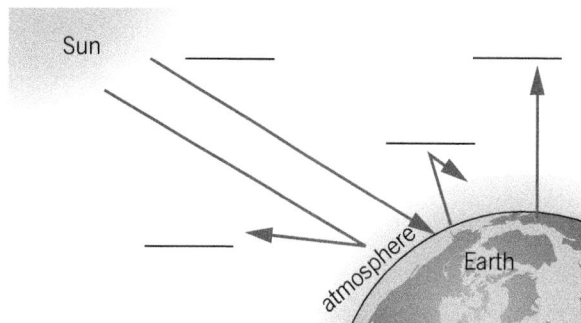

C Explain the meanings of the phrases below.

a Greenhouse effect

_____

_____

_____

b Global warming

_____

_____

_____

D The statements below are about the graph. Tick the statements that are **true**.

1 The graph shows that the concentration of
carbon dioxide in the atmosphere has
increased since 1800. ☐

2 The graph shows that in 1964 the concentration
of carbon dioxide was about 320 parts
per million. ☐

3 The graph shows that the concentration of carbon
dioxide in the atmosphere will continue to rise in future. ☐

4 The graph shows that increasing concentrations
of carbon dioxide cause global warming. ☐

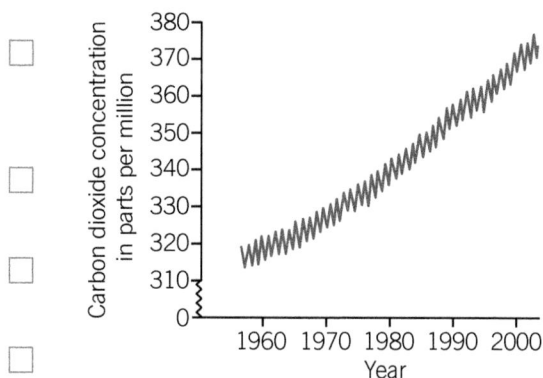

7.3.2 The carbon cycle

A Fill in the gaps to complete the sentences.

There are several carbon stores, or _____. These include the atmosphere, the ocean, some

_____ rocks, _____ fuels, plants and animals, and the soil. The carbon

_____ shows how carbon atoms are recycled when they move between stores. For example, carbon

dioxide enters the atmosphere when plants and animals _____. It also enters the atmosphere when

fossil fuels _____. Carbon dioxide leaves the atmosphere when plants use it in _____.

It also leaves the atmosphere by _____ in oceans. Before industrialisation, carbon dioxide was added

to the atmosphere at the _____ rate as it left the atmosphere. This meant that the concentration of

carbon dioxide did not _____.

B The diagram below shows the carbon cycle.

In each box, write the name of the correct carbon sink (also called a carbon store or carbon reservoir).

Along each arrow, write the name of the correct **one** or **two** processes from the box below.

combustion	**respiration**	**decay in absence of oxygen**	**photosynthesis**
	dissolving	**rock formation**	**coming out of solution**

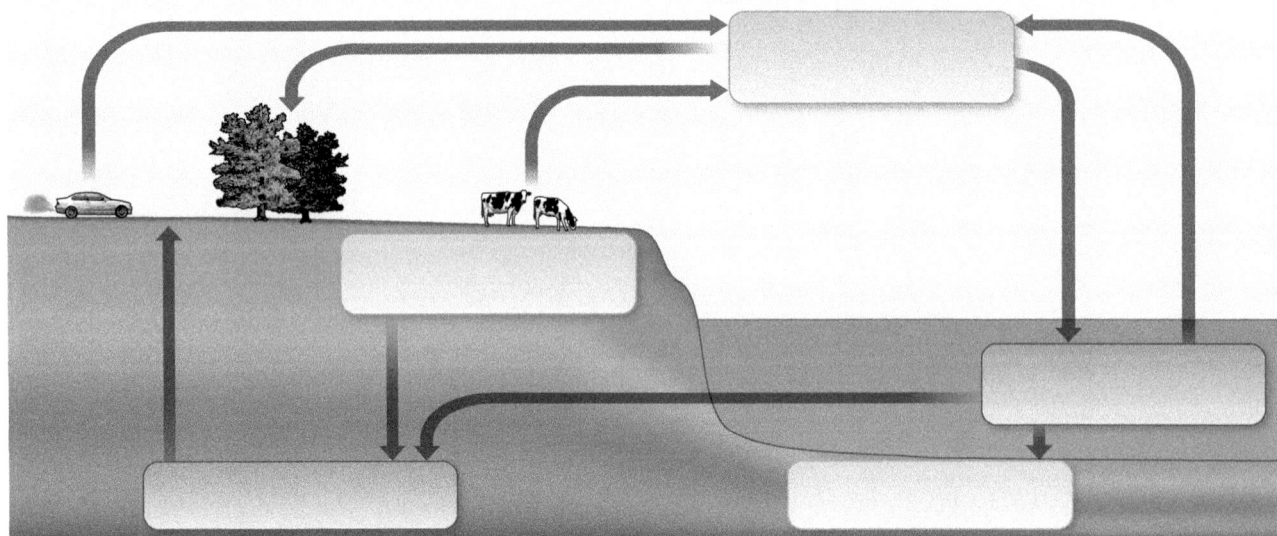

C Use the carbon cycle to help you to complete the sentences below.

a For many years, the concentration of carbon dioxide in the atmosphere remained constant because

_____

_____

b Since industrialisation, the concentration of carbon dioxide in the atmosphere has increased because

_____

_____

c This word equation: carbon dioxide + water → glucose + oxygen shows one way in which carbon dioxide is removed

_____

7.3.3 Climate change

A Fill in the gaps to complete the sentences.

Human activities affect the carbon _____. For example, burning fossil fuels increases the

concentration of _____ dioxide in the atmosphere. This extra carbon dioxide causes an increase in the

air _____ at the surface of the Earth. This is global _____. Global _____

makes glaciers and polar _____ melt. Global warming also causes climate change, which is a

change to long-term _____ patterns. Examples of climate change include more frequent droughts

and heatwaves in some areas, and more rainfall in other areas. Climate change leads to some animal and plant

_____ becoming extinct and may make it harder for humans to grow enough _____.

B Draw a line to match each cause to one direct effect.

Cause	**Effect**
Deforestation	More carbon dioxide goes into the atmosphere
Burning fossil fuels	The concentration of carbon dioxide in the atmosphere increases
Every year, more carbon dioxide is added to the atmosphere than is removed	Less carbon dioxide is removed from the atmosphere
Climate change	Glaciers melt, some plant and animal species become extinct, it is harder for humans in some areas to grow enough food

C Write the number of each statement below in the correct column of the table.
1 Experiments show that burning fossil fuels makes carbon dioxide gas.
2 Intensive farming leads to the release of a greenhouse gas, methane.
3 In some areas, global warming causes more frequent flooding.
4 The Earth's orbit changes over time. When the Earth is nearer the Sun, the climate is warmer.
5 Scientists have shown that erupting volcanoes give out carbon dioxide.
6 Experiments show that carbon dioxide molecules store energy.
7 When people cut down large areas of forests, there are fewer trees to remove carbon dioxide from the atmosphere.
8 In some areas, global warming causes more frequent droughts.

Evidence that human activity causes climate change	Evidence that climate change occurs naturally	Statements that do not provide evidence about the causes of climate change

D Cows produce large amounts of two greenhouse gases, carbon dioxide and methane. A government suggests reducing greenhouse gas emissions by banning people from eating meat from cattle.
Evaluate the implications of this suggestion.

_____

_____

_____

_____

_____

Hint: In your answer, describe the benefits and disadvantages of the idea. Then write down whether or not – overall – you think the suggestion is a good idea.

7.4.1 Extracting metals

A Fill in the gaps to complete the sentences.

Most metals exist in the Earth's _____ as compounds. These compounds are _____

with other compounds in rock. A rock that it is worth extracting a metal from is called an _____.

Metals that are _____ carbon in the reactivity series can be extracted from their compounds by

heating with carbon. Metals that are above carbon in the reactivity series are extracted from their compounds by

_____.

B Draw a tick next to each metal that you predict can be extracted from its ore by heating with carbon. Then use the reactivity series on this page to explain each prediction.

Part of the reactivity series, including carbon (a non-metal)	
calcium	**most reactive**
magnesium	
aluminium	
carbon	
zinc	
iron	
lead	**least reactive**
copper	

Metal	✔ if it can be extracted by heating with carbon	Scientific explanation of prediction
zinc		
magnesium		
lead		

C Aluminium is extracted from its ore by electrolysis. When a company finds an aluminium ore deposit, the manager must decide whether it is worth mining the ore and extracting aluminium from it. Below are some quantities the manager must take into account.

- The percentage of aluminium in the ore.
- The mass of solid waste produced when 1 kg of aluminium oxide is separated from the ore.
- The distance from the mine to a place where electrolysis can take place.
- The mass of greenhouse gases made when the electricity is generated.

a Suggest **two** economic factors that the manager must take into account when deciding whether or not to mine the ore and extract aluminium from it. Do not choose factors from the list.

> **Hint:** Economic factors are those to do with money.

_____

_____

b Suggest **one** way in which the mass of solid waste from the extraction process can be reduced.

_____

c Electrolysis uses lots of electricity. Suggest **one** way to reduce the amount of carbon dioxide made during electricity production.

_____

7.4.2 Recycling

A Fill in the gaps to complete the sentences.

Recycling means collecting and _____ used materials so that they can be used again. There are

many advantages of recycling, including _____ the need to extract resources.

B The statements below can be reordered to describe how aluminium is recycled. Read the statements and write down the order of statements you think will give the best description.

Correct order: ☐ ☐ ☐ ☐ ☐ ☐

1 Use a lorry to collect used cans.

2 Pour the liquid aluminium into a mould.

3 Leave the liquid aluminium to cool and freeze.

4 Melt the shreds of aluminium in a furnace.

5 Shred the cans.

6 Use magnets to separate aluminium cans from steel cans.

C Evaluate the advantages and disadvantages of recycling aluminium compared to extracting the metal from its ore.

Hint: Start by giving some advantages and disadvantages of recycling aluminium compared to extracting the metal from its ore. Then discuss whether or not you think that, overall, it is worth recycling aluminium.

_____

_____

_____

_____

_____

_____

D Many types of plastic can be recycled. However, there are many advantages of reducing the amount of plastic that is used in the first place.

a Suggest **two** advantages of reducing the total amount of plastic that people use.

_____

_____

_____

_____

b Suggest **two** ways of reducing the total amount of plastic that people use.

_____

_____

_____

_____

Big Idea 7 Pinchpoint ⧖

Pinchpoint question

Answer the question below, then do the follow-up activity **with the same letter** as the answer you picked.

Which metals can be extracted by heating their naturally occurring compounds with carbon, and why?

Use the reactivity series to help you.

A Chromium and nickel, because they are less reactive than carbon.

B Rubidium and beryllium, because they are less reactive than carbon.

C Beryllium and chromium, because their reactivities are similar to the reactivity of carbon.

D Barium and strontium, because they are more reactive than carbon.

Reactivity series	
rubidium	↑ **most reactive**
potassium	
barium	
strontium	
beryllium	
carbon	
chromium	
nickel	
copper	**least reactive**

Follow-up activities

A A metal that is less reactive than carbon may be extracted from its compound by heating the compound with carbon. Carbon displaces the metal from its compound. Some metals are extracted from their compounds in displacement reactions with elements other than carbon.

The displacement reactions below are all used to extract metals from their compounds.
For each displacement reaction, circle the name of the **more** reactive metal (or non-metal) in the word equation. Then balance the symbol equation.

a titanium chloride + sodium → titanium + sodium chloride

$TiCl_4 + \underline{\quad}Na \rightarrow Ti + \underline{\quad}NaCl$

b chromium oxide + aluminium → aluminium oxide + chromium

$Cr_2O_3 + \underline{\quad}Al \rightarrow Al_2O_3 + \underline{\quad}Cr$

c tungsten oxide + hydrogen → tungsten + water

$WO_3 + \underline{\quad}H_2 \rightarrow W + \underline{\quad}H_2O$

Hint: When balancing a chemical equation, do not change any of the chemical formulae. For help, see 6.3.4 Conservation of mass and 7.4.1 Extracting metals.

B If a metal is **less** reactive than carbon, it may be extracted from its compound by heating the compound with carbon. The reactivity series lists metals in order of their reactivity.

In each list below, use a pen to draw a circle around the **most** reactive metal and use a pencil to draw a circle around the **least** reactive metal. Use the reactivity series on the page opposite to help you.

a rubidium   nickel   strontium   **d** potassium   rubidium   strontium

b chromium   barium   potassium   **e** copper   nickel   chromium

c copper   beryllium   barium

Hint: Copper is the least reactive metal in the reactivity series shown on the opposite page. What does this tell you about the order of metals in the reactivity series? For help, see 7.4.1 Extracting metals.

C Draw one line from each sentence starter to its correct ending. Use each ending once, more than once, or not at all. You will need to refer to the reactivity series in the Pinchpoint question.

	1 because it is a metal.
a In the reactivity series, metals are listed in order of	**2** increasing reactivity from top to bottom.
b Carbon can be included in the reactivity series	**3** if the metal is less reactive than carbon.
c Carbon may displace a metal from its compounds	**4** decreasing reactivity from top to bottom.
d Carbon may be used to extract a metal from its compounds	**5** even though it is not a metal.
	6 if the metal is more reactive than carbon.

Hint: Which is more reactive, potassium or copper? Where are these metals in the reactivity series opposite? What does this tell you about the order of metals in the reactivity series? For help, see 7.4.1 Extracting metals.

D Some of the sentences and word equations below include one or more mistakes.
Read the sentences and correct the mistakes.

The reactivity series lists metals in order of reactivity. Metals at the bottom are more reactive than metals at the top.

Carbon is also included in the reactivity series, even though it is not a metal.

If a metal is above carbon in the reactivity series, it is less reactive than carbon.

A metal that is more reactive than carbon may be extracted from its compounds by heating with carbon.
A decomposition reaction occurs.

The word equations below show examples of displacement reactions in which a metal is extracted from a compound by heating with hydrogen:

tin oxide + carbon → tin oxide + carbon dioxide

lead oxide + carbon dioxide → lead + carbon dioxide

Hint: Copper can be extracted from its compounds by heating with carbon. What does this tell you about the position in the reactivity series of metals that can be extracted by heating with carbon? For help, see 7.4.1 Extracting metals.

Pinchpoint review
Now look back at the question – do you think you chose the right letter?
Turn to the Answers page to find out.

Section 2 Revision questions

1 ⚗️⚗️ Complete the table below. *(5 marks)*

Element name	Chemical symbol
Carbon	
Chlorine	
	Na
Iron	
	W

2 ⚗️⚗️ Draw a line to match each particle diagram to its description. *(3 marks)*

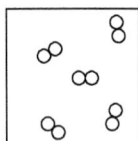

Particle diagram	Description
	a mixture of two compounds
	a pure element
	a mixture of two elements
	a mixture of an element and a compound

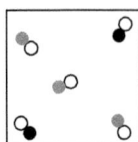

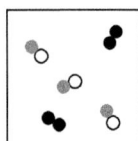

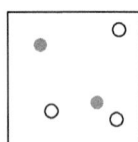

3 ⚗️⚗️ Gallium arsenide is a compound that is used in electronic devices. It is also used in some solar cells.

a Define the term 'compound'. *(1 mark)*

_____

_____

b The formula of gallium arsenide is GaAs. Use the Periodic table at the back of the book to name the two elements whose atoms are in the compound. *(1 mark)*

_____ and _____

c Gallium arsenide is made in a chemical reaction between the two elements you named in part **b**. Write a word equation for the reaction. *(1 mark)*

_____

4 ⚗️⚗️ Caffeine is a substance that is in tea, coffee, and chocolate. It makes people feel more alert, and quickens the heart rate.
The chemical formula of caffeine is $C_8H_{10}N_4O_2$.

a Write how many different **types** of atom are in a caffeine molecule. *(1 mark)*

_____

b Calculate the total number of atoms in a caffeine molecule. Show your working. *(2 marks)*

_____

_____

5 ⚗️⚗️ The formula of silver sulfide is Ag_2S.

a Explain what this formula shows. *(2 marks)*

_____

_____

_____

_____

b At room temperature, sulfur is a yellow solid and silver sulfide is a black solid.
Explain why the properties of silver sulfide are different from the properties of silver and sulfur. *(1 mark)*

_____

_____

_____

_____

_____

_____

6 ⚗️⚗️ Many barbecues use charcoal as a fuel. Charcoal is mainly carbon. Carbon burns in air to make carbon dioxide, which is in the gas state at room temperature.

a Suggest whether the burning reaction is exothermic or endothermic, and explain your decision. *(1 mark)*

_____

_____

b Predict whether the mass of solid on the barbecue will increase, decrease, or stay the same. Explain your answer. *(2 marks)*

_____

_____

_____

_____

_____

7 🧪🧪 The concentration of carbon dioxide in the atmosphere did not change for many years, but has changed greatly since the 1960s. Explain why. (*6 marks*)

Hint: In your answer, name the processes that add carbon dioxide to the atmosphere, and the processes that remove them.

_____

_____

_____

_____

_____

_____

_____

_____

_____

_____

8 🧪🧪 Describe and explain **two** impacts of global warming. (*4 marks*)

_____

_____

_____

_____

_____

_____

_____

_____

9 🧪🧪 Zinc is extracted from its ore.

a 500 kg of zinc ore is extracted from a mine in China. The ore contains 45 kg of zinc.

Calculate the percentage of zinc in the ore. (*2 marks*)

_____ %

b In Europe, zinc used to be extracted from its oxide by heating with carbon monoxide. The equation for the reaction is: $ZnO + CO \rightarrow Zn + CO_2$

i Name the product that is formed in the gas state. (*1 mark*)

_____

ii Suggest why this process is not now used in Europe. (*1 mark*)

_____

_____

10 🧪🧪🧪 **Table 1** shows some data for the Group 3 elements. The elements are listed in the same order as they are in the Periodic Table.

Table 1

Element	Density (g/cm³)
boron	2.34
aluminium	2.70
gallium	5.91
indium	
thallium	11.8

a Describe the trend in density from top to bottom of Group 3. (*1 mark*)

_____

_____

b Predict the density of indium.

_____ g/cm³ (*1 mark*)

c Explain how you made your prediction in part **b**. (*1 mark*)

_____

_____

_____

11 🧪🧪🧪 Lithium nitrate decomposes on heating. The word equation shows the reaction.

lithium nitrate →

lithium oxide + nitrogen dioxide + oxygen

a Explain how the word equation shows that the reaction is a decomposition reaction. (*1 mark*)

_____

_____

b A teacher wanted to demonstrate the decomposition reaction of lithium nitrate at school. He looked up the hazard symbols for nitrogen dioxide gas. Two of these are shown in **Figure 1**.

Figure 1

Use the hazard symbols to suggest why the teacher decided not to do the demonstration.

(2 marks)

_____

_____

_____

_____

_____

_____

c A university student took suitable safety precautions. She placed 2.76 g of lithium nitrate in an open test tube and heated strongly. When the chemical reaction finished, the mass of solid lithium oxide in the test tube was 0.60 g.

i Use the particle model to explain why the nitrogen dioxide gas and oxygen gas that were made in the reaction escaped from the test tube.

(2 marks)

_____

_____

_____

_____

_____

_____

ii Calculate the total mass of nitrogen dioxide gas and oxygen gas that were made in the reaction. Show your working. *(2 marks)*

_____

_____

d Balance the formula equation for the decomposition reaction by writing one number on each answer line.

$4LiNO_3 \rightarrow$ _____ $Li_2O +$ _____ $NO_2 + O_2$ *(1 mark)*

12 In 4 g of helium, there are 600 000 million million million atoms. Estimate the number of atoms in a balloon that contains 0.4 g of helium. *(2 marks)*

_____

13 Lithium reacts with oxygen gas to make lithium oxide, which is in the solid state at room temperature. Write a balanced symbol equation for the reaction. Use the formulae below and include state symbols.

Formulae: Li O_2 Li_2O *(2 marks)*

Hint: When balancing chemical equations, do not change the formulae.

_____

14 **Table 2** and **Table 3** give data for one physical property of the elements in Group 1 and Group 0 of the Periodic Table. The elements are listed in the same order in the Periodic Table.

Table 2

Group 1 element	Melting point (°C)
lithium	180
sodium	98
potassium	64
rubidium	39

Table 3

Group 0 element	Melting point (°C)
helium	−270
neon	−249
argon	−189
krypton	−157

Use data from **Table 2** and **Table 3**, and your own knowledge, to compare the patterns in two physical properties and one chemical property of the elements in Group 1 and Group 0. *(6 marks)*

_____

_____

_____

_____

_____

_____

_____

_____

_____

_____

Section 2 Checklist

Revision question number	Outcome	Topic reference	☹	😐	☺
1	Correctly write down the chemical symbols of four elements and, given chemical symbols, write down their names.	5.3.1			
2	Interpret particle diagrams to identify elements, compounds, and different types of mixtures.	5.3.3			
3a	State what a compound is.	5.3.3			
3b	Given chemical formulae, name the elements present and their relative proportions.	5.3.4			
3c	Write word equations from information about chemical reactions.	6.3.2			
4a, b	Interpret chemical formulae.	5.3.4			
5a	Interpret chemical formulae.	5.3.4			
5b	Explain why a compound has different properties from those of the elements whose atoms it contains.	5.3.3			
6a	Recognise that burning reactions are exothermic.	6.4.1			
6b	Explain observations about mass in a chemical change.	6.3.4			
7	Explain why the concentration of carbon dioxide in the atmosphere did not change for many years.	7.3.2			
8	Describe how global warming can impact on climate and local weather patterns.	7.3.3			
9a	Calculate the percentage by mass of a metal in its ore.	7.4.1 🧮			
9b	Interpret information about extracting a metal from its ore.	7.4.1			
10a	Use data to describe a trend in physical properties.	5.4.1 🧮			
10b	Use data showing a pattern in physical properties to predict the missing value for an element.	5.4.1 🧮			
10c	Explain how to predict missing data values using trends in properties.	5.4.1			
11a	Explain why a given reaction is an example of combustion or thermal decomposition.	6.3.3			
11b	Identify risks, hazards and control measures in a demonstration.	6.3.1			
11c	Explain observations about mass in a chemical or physical change.	6.3.4			
11d	Use known masses of reactants or products to calculate unknown masses of the remaining reactant or product	6.3.4			
11e	Balance a symbol equation.	6.3.4			
12	Estimate the number of atoms in a sample.	5.3.2 🧮			
13	Balance a symbol equation.	6.3.4 🧮			
14	Use data about the properties of elements to identify patterns, similarities, and differences.	5.4.2 5.4.4			

8.3.1 Gas exchange

A Fill in the gaps to complete the sentences.

Breathing is carried out by the _____ system and the major organs of this system are your

_____. When you inhale you take in _____ into the blood and when you

_____ you give out carbon dioxide from the blood. When you inhale, air travels in through

your mouth and nose and then through your _____. It then travels into your lungs through the

_____ and then through a bronchiole, finally moving into an air sac called an _____.

These have thin walls and create a large surface area for _____ _____, which means

that the gases can diffuse in and out of the blood easily.

B Label the diagram of the human respiratory system.

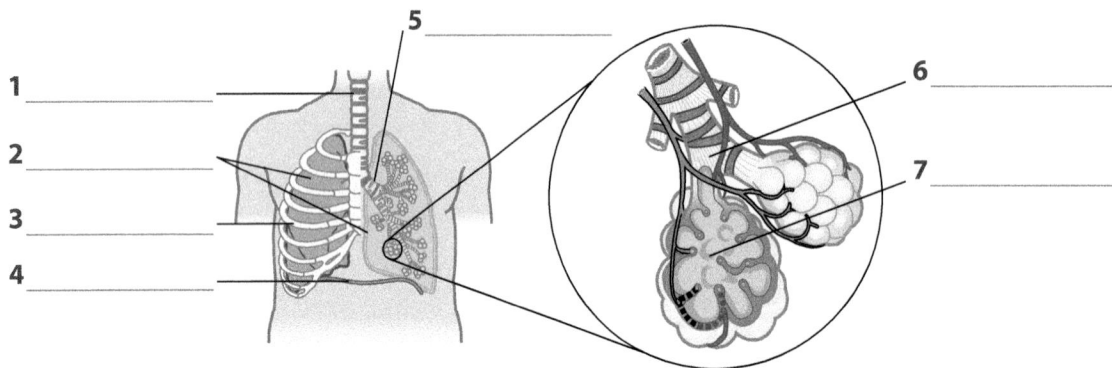

C There are millions of alveoli in the lungs. Explain how they are adapted for gas exchange.

_____

_____

_____

D These pie charts show the difference in composition of inhaled and exhaled air.

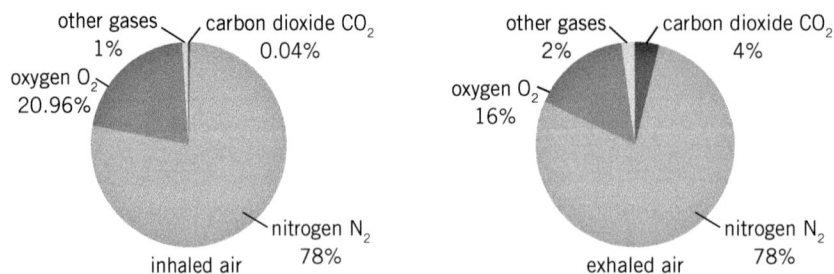

other gases 1%   carbon dioxide CO_2 0.04%
oxygen O_2 20.96%
nitrogen N_2 78%
inhaled air

other gases 2%   carbon dioxide CO_2 4%
oxygen O_2 16%
nitrogen N_2 78%
exhaled air

Use the data to describe and explain the differences between the gases in inhaled and exhaled air.

a Carbon dioxide _____

_____

b Oxygen _____

_____

c Nitrogen _____

_____

8.3.2 Breathing

A Fill in the gaps to complete the sentences.

When you inhale, the muscles between your _____ and your diaphragm _____.

This _____ the volume of your chest cavity which _____ the pressure, causing

air to be drawn in. When you exhale, the muscles _____; this _____ the volume

of your chest cavity. This _____ the pressure and forces air _____. You can use a

_____ to model this process. Smoking and diseases such as _____ can reduce

lung _____.

B Explain how the actions of the ribcage and diaphragm cause you to inhale.

_____

_____

_____

_____

C A bell jar model can be used to model what happens during breathing.

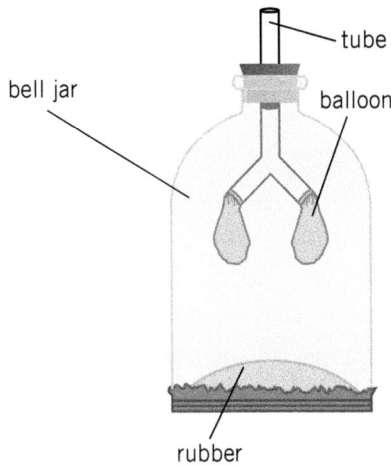

a Describe how the model can be used to represent what happens when you exhale.

_____

_____

_____

b Describe **one** limitation of this model.

_____

D Explain how you can use the equipment shown to measure your lung volume.

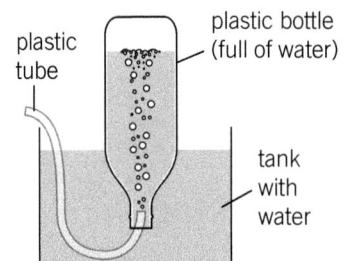

_____

_____

_____

_____

8.3.3 Drugs

A Fill in the gaps to complete the sentences.

Chemicals that affect the way your body works are called _____. _____ drugs are

taken for enjoyment whereas _____ drugs benefit your health. If you regularly take a drug, you

may develop an _____. If you then try to stop taking the drug, you may suffer from unpleasant

_____ _____, which make it harder to give up.

B Drugs can be divided into two main categories – medicinal and recreational drugs.
Describe what is meant by each type of drug and give a named example.

   a   Medicinal drug _____

       Example _____

   b   Recreational drug _____

       Example _____

C Complete the following sentences to describe how each of the following drugs affects your health.

   a   Alcohol – damages _____

   b   Tobacco – increases risk of _____ cancer

   c   Caffeine – _____ the nervous system

D Explain why people take the following medicinal drugs.

   a   Antibiotic _____

   b   Paracetamol _____

E If your body gets used to the changes caused by a drug, you can become an addict.
Explain **two** problems associated with addiction to a recreational drug

   1 _____

      _____

   2 _____

      _____

8.3.4 Alcohol

A Fill in the gaps to complete the sentences.

Alcoholic drinks contain the drug _____. This acts on the _____ system and

slows down body reactions; it is called a _____. Drinking too much alcohol can result in

_____ and brain damage. Different alcoholic drinks contain different amounts of alcohol. 10 ml of

alcohol is known as one _____ of alcohol. The government recommends that adults drink less than

2–3 units a day to remain healthy. People who are addicted to alcohol are known as _____.

B Long-term use of alcohol can lead to death.

a Name the main two organs that are damaged by drinking alcohol.

1 _____

2 _____

b The graph shows the number of alcohol-related deaths in UK males between 1991 and 2008.

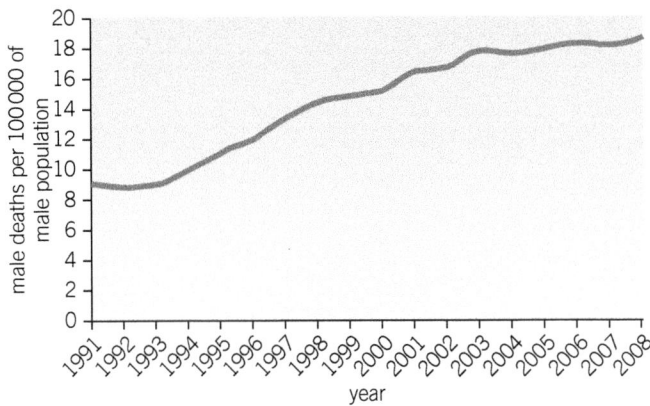

Using data from the graph, describe the trend shown.

_____

_____

_____

C Alcohol has an effect on pregnancy and conception.

a Explain why men should reduce their alcohol intake if they are planning to have a child.

_____

_____

b Explain why a pregnant woman should avoid alcohol.

_____

_____

_____

8.3.5 Smoking

A Fill in the gaps to complete the sentences.

Smoking increases the risk of many conditions such as lung _____ and _____ attacks.

The risk of someone else developing one of these conditions also increases if they breathe in the smoke. This is

called _____ smoking. Tobacco smoke contains many harmful chemicals such as tar which narrows

the _____, carbon _____ which reduces the amount of _____ the

blood can carry, and nicotine. As well as being addictive, nicotine is a _____ which makes the heart

beat faster. Smoking in pregnancy affects foetal development and can cause _____.

B Tobacco smoke contains over 4000 chemicals, many of which are harmful.
Describe the effects of the following components of tobacco smoke on the body.

   a   Tar _____

   b   Carbon monoxide _____

   c   Nicotine _____

C Carlos studies the graph opposite.

He draws a conclusion based on the data: If you smoke then you will get lung cancer.

Correct his conclusion.

_____

_____

_____

_____

_____

_____

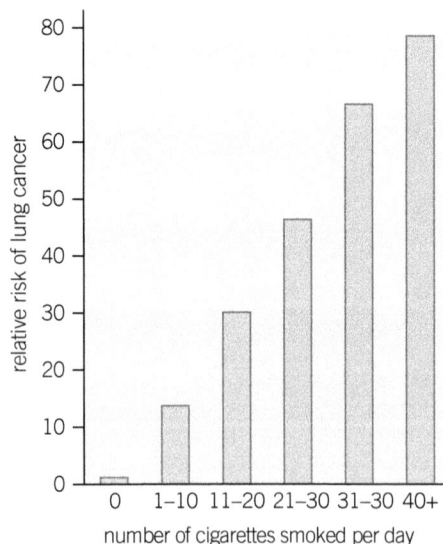

relative risk of lung cancer (y-axis: 0 to 80)
number of cigarettes smoked per day (x-axis: 0, 1–10, 11–20, 21–30, 31–30, 40+)

D Explain how smoking increases your risk of suffering from a respiratory infection.

_____

_____

_____

Hint: Think about the ciliated cells in your airways.

E Explain why a pregnant woman should avoid smoking.

_____

8.4.1 Nutrients

A Fill in the gaps to complete the sentences.

To remain healthy you must eat a _____ diet. This means eating food containing the right

_____ in the right amounts. These include _____ and _____ which

give you energy, _____ for growth and repair, _____ and _____ to

keep you healthy, and water and _____ to keep the food moving through your gut.

B Complete the table to explain the role of each nutrient in the body.

Nutrient	Role in the body
Carbohydrate	
Lipid	
Protein	
Vitamins and minerals	

C Fibre is not a nutrient. Explain why it is still an essential part of a healthy diet.

_____

_____

_____

D The food labels below are taken from a pizza and a tin of baked beans.

NUTRITION INFORMATION

Typical Composition	A 175g (6¼ oz) Serving Provides	100g (3½ oz) Provide
Energy	1567kJ/372kcal	893kJ/212kcal
Protein	20.2g	11.5g
Carbohydrate of which sugars	47.6g 7.7g	27.1g 4.4g
Fat of which saturates mono-unsaturates polyunsaturates	11.2g 6.3g 3.7g 1.1g	6.4g 3.6g 2.1g 0.6g
Fibre	3.3g	1.9g
Sodium	0.8g	0.5g

PIZZA

NUTRITION INFORMATION

Typical Values	Amount per 100g	Amount per Can
Energy	312kJ/75kcal	468kJ/113kcal
Protein	4.7g	7.1g
Carbohydrate (of which sugars)	13.6g (6.0g)	20.4g (9.0g)
Fat (of which saturates)	0.2g (Trace)	0.3g (Trace)
Fibre	3.7g	5.6g
Sodium	0.5g	0.7g

BAKED BEANS in tomato sauce

For an average person, which would be the healthier choice? _____

Give 3 reasons for your answer.

1 _____

2 _____

3 _____

8.4.2 Food tests

A Fill in the gaps to complete the sentences.

Scientists use _____ _____ to find out which nutrients are present in a food product.

_____ turns blue-black when _____ is present. Benedict's solution turns orange-

_____ if sugar is present. A solution of copper sulfate and sodium hydroxide solution will turn

_____ if _____ is present. Ethanol will turn _____ if lipids are present.

B Complete the table to show the chemical which should be used to test for the presence of each nutrient in a food solution.

Nutrient	Chemical
Starch	
	Ethanol
	Benedict's solution
Protein	

C You can also test a solid food sample for the presence of lipids. Describe this process.

_____

_____

_____

D A student tested three unknown food samples for the presence of different nutrients.

Sample	Colour of solution after adding...			
	Iodine	Benedict's solution	Ethanol	Copper sulfate and sodium hydroxide
X	Blue-black	Blue	Clear	Purple
Y	Orange-yellow	Red	Cloudy	Purple
Z	Orange-yellow	Red	Cloudy	Pale blue

Look at the results in the table and answer the following questions.

a Name which sample or samples contain protein. _____

b Name which sample or samples contain lipids. _____

c List the nutrients found in sample **Z**. _____

d Name which sample is most likely to be milk, and explain why. _____

Reasons: _____

e Give **one** reason why testing food for the presence of nutrients is important.

_____

8.4.3 Unhealthy diet

A Fill in the gaps to complete the sentences.

Eating the wrong amount or wrong types of food is called _____. If the energy in the food you eat is

less than the energy you use, you will lose body mass and become _____. You are also likely not to

take in the correct amount of a vitamin or mineral. This is called a _____ and can make you ill.

Not eating enough food for prolonged periods is called _____. If you take in more energy than

you use by eating too much, you will gain body mass as _____, which is stored under the skin.

Extremely overweight people are said to be _____.

B Describe **two** conditions you are more likely to suffer from if you are underweight.

1 _____

2 _____

C Describe **two** conditions you are more likely to suffer from if you are overweight.

1 _____

2 _____

D The table below shows the energy requirements of some males and females.

Gender	Energy requirement per day (kJ)				
	Child	**Teenager**	**Office worker**	**Construction worker**	**Pregnant woman**
Male	8000	10 000	10 000	15 000	–
Female	8000	9000	9000	13 000	11 000

a i Calculate the difference in the amount of energy required by a male construction worker, and a male who works in an office job.

_____ kJ

ii Explain this difference.

_____

_____

b i Calculate the percentage increase in a female office worker's energy needs due to pregnancy.

_____ %

ii Explain this difference.

_____

_____

E Explain how an unhealthy diet can lead to obesity.

_____

_____

_____

8.4.4 Digestive system

A Fill in the gaps to complete the sentences.

The group of organs that work together to break down food are called the _____ _____.

Food enters the mouth and travels down your _____ into your _____. Here it is mixed with

_____ and digestive juices. As a result of _____ small molecules of nutrients are produced

which pass through the villi in the _____ intestine into the blood. Water passes back into the body in

the _____ intestine leaving undigested food called faeces. This is stored in the _____ until it

leaves the body through the _____.

B Label the diagram of the digestive system.

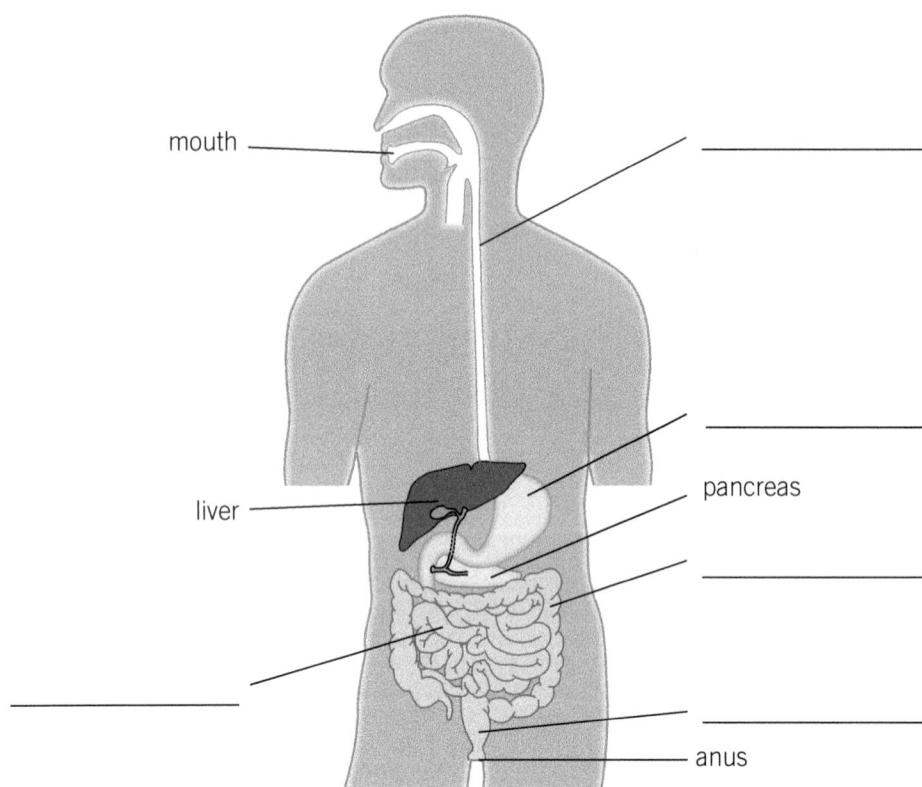

mouth

pancreas

liver

anus

C Describe the function of the following organs in the digestive system.

Stomach _____

Large intestine _____

D Explain **two** ways the small intestine is adapted to its function.

1 _____

2 _____

E Explain why food needs to be digested.

_____

_____

_____

8.4.5 Bacteria and enzymes in digestion

A Fill in the gaps to complete the sentences.

Some gut _____ living in your large intestine help you to remain healthy by making _____.

Special proteins called _____ help speed up digestion without being used up. They are a type

of _____. There are three main types – _____ which breaks down carbohydrate

molecules into _____ molecules, _____ which breaks down _____

into amino acids and _____ which breaks down lipid molecules into fatty acids and _____.

To help further with lipid digestion, _____ breaks the lipids into smaller droplets that are easier for

the enzymes to work on.

B a Identify the **two** correct statements about enzymes.

W They are made of lipids.

X They speed up digestion.

Y They are known as biological catalysts.

Z They are used up during a reaction.

b Rewrite the **two** incorrect statements, so they read correctly.

_____

_____

C Each type of enzyme is involved in a different reaction. Complete the table to link the type of enzyme to the molecule it breaks down, and the molecules that are produced

Enzyme	Molecule it breaks down	Molecules produced
carbohydrase		
	lipid	
		amino acids

D There are some bacteria that live in your digestive system and improve your health.

a Name where these bacteria are found.

_____

b Name the food source for these bacteria.

_____

c Explain how they improve your health.

_____

_____

Pinchpoint question

Answer the question below, then do the follow-up activity **with the same letter** as the answer you picked.

Which of the following statements best describes the structure and function of the small intestine?

A Villi present in the small intestine move food particles along the intestine, speeding up absorption.

B The small intestine is specially adapted for its sole function of absorption, so enzymes are not present.

C The small intestine has a large surface area to maximise the rate of absorption.

D The wall of the small intestine is smooth to maximise the rate of absorption.

Follow-up activities

A Circle the correct bold terms in the sentences below to describe how food is moved along the intestine.

Fat / fibre in your food is not digested. This adds **liquid / bulk** to the food.

Muscles / ligaments in the **wall / centre** of the intestine **push against / pull** this mass, forcing the food along the intestine.

This process can be modelled by **sucking on a straw / squeezing a tube of toothpaste**.

Small **soluble / insoluble** molecules produced as a result of digestion are absorbed through the **small / large** intestine wall into the blood stream. The villi present increase the surface area of the small intestine. This **prevents / speeds up** absorption.

Eventually only a solid mass of undigested food is left. This is called **urine / feces** which is stored in the **rectum / bladder** until it can be removed from the body.

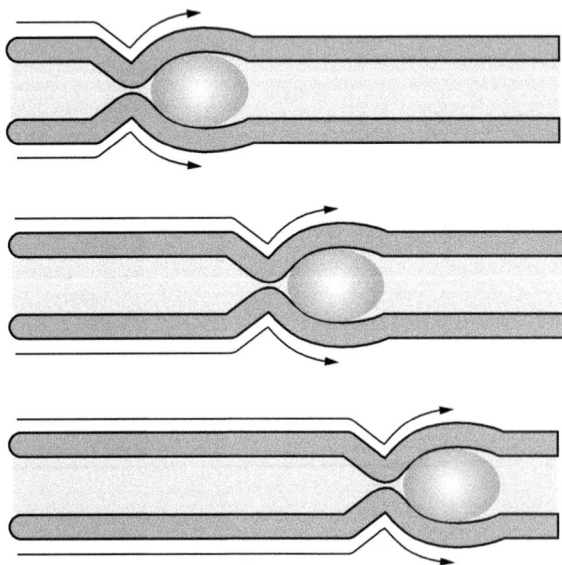

Hint: Look at the diagram to help you complete the sentences. For help, see 8.4.4 Digestive system.

B Enzymes in the body help to digest large food molecules. There are three main groups of enzymes.

a Complete the following sentences to describe the role of each enzyme.

Carbohydrase enzymes break down _____ into _____

Protease enzymes break down _____ into _____

Lipase enzymes break down _____ into _____

b Complete the following table to show where enzymes are found in the body. Add a tick for each place the enzyme is found.

Enzyme	Mouth	Stomach	Small intestine
Carbohydrase			
Protease			
Lipase			

Hint: There is only one type of enzyme found in the mouth. It breaks down large carbohydrate molecules into sugars. For help, see 8.4.5 Bacteria and enzymes in digestion.

C Coeliac disease is caused by an abnormal immune system reaction to the protein gluten, which is found in foods such as bread, pasta, cereals and biscuits. It causes the immune system to mistake healthy cells and substances for harmful ones and produces antibodies against them (antibodies usually fight off bacteria and viruses). The antibodies produced for people with coeliac disease cause the surface of their intestine to become inflamed. This inflammation flattens villi, reducing their ability to help with digestion.

a Name the main food group that includes foods containing gluten.

_____

b Suggest and explain the symptoms of coeliac disease.

_____

_____

_____

_____

Hint: Think about the function of villi. What would happen if the villi were removed? For help, see 8.4.4 Digestive system.

D The wall of the small intestine is covered in tiny projections called villi.

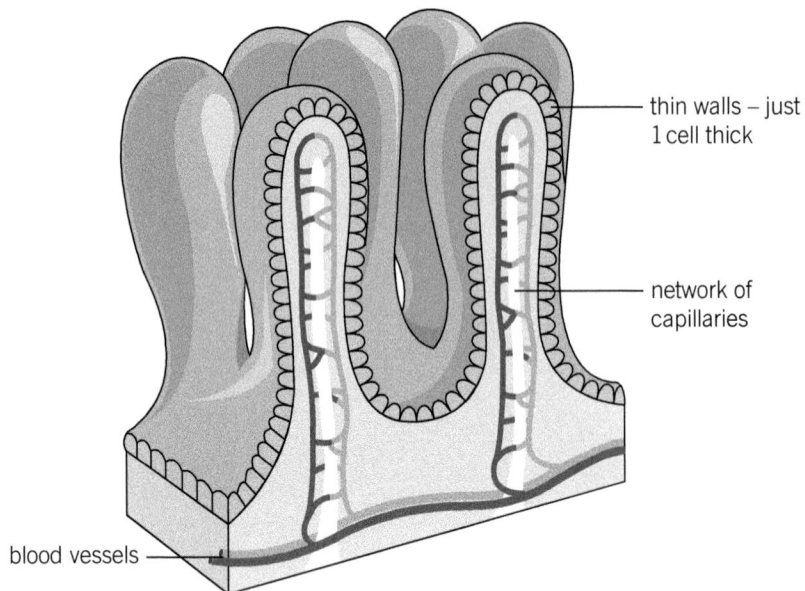

thin walls – just
1 cell thick

network of
capillaries

blood vessels

a Draw a line to match each sentence starter to its correct ending.

i Walls of intestine are thin	**1** to create a large surface area.

ii Walls of intestine are covered in lots of villi	**2** to transport absorbed food molecules to where they are needed.

iii Villi have a rich blood supply	**3** to minimise the diffusion distance.

b Explain how a constant flow of blood through the villi maximises diffusion.

_____

_____

_____

Hint: The rate of diffusion is affected by distance, the difference in concentration and the surface area in contact. For help, see 8.4.4 Digestive system.

Pinchpoint review
Now look back at the question – do you think you chose the right letter?
Turn to the Answers page to find out.

9.3.1 Aerobic respiration

A Fill in the gaps to complete the sentences.

Energy is released in your cells by _____ _____. During this process, _____

and oxygen react inside your _____ to release energy. The waste products carbon dioxide and

_____ are also produced.

Glucose is produced when _____ are broken down during digestion. Glucose is transported around

your body in the _____ in the blood. It then _____ into cells.

Oxygen is also transported by the blood. It binds to the _____ in red blood cells.

B Complete the word equation for aerobic respiration.

glucose + _____ ⟶ water _____ + _____ (+ energy)

C Respiration takes place inside your cells.

a Name the component of the cell in which respiration occurs. _____

b Explain why muscle cells contain large numbers of this component.

_____

_____

D Imagine you have been asked to plan an investigation to measure the effect of exercise on breathing rates.

a List the following variables in your investigation:

i independent variable _____

ii dependent variable _____

iii control variable _____

b Explain what you think will happen.

_____

_____

_____

E Explain how the following reactants of aerobic respiration get into your cells.

Include the key words below in your answer.

| diffuse | alveoli | plasma | haemoglobin |

a glucose

_____

_____

_____

b oxygen

_____

_____

_____

9.3.2 Anaerobic respiration

A Fill in the gaps to complete the sentences.

When your body respires without oxygen it is called _____ _____. This produces

_____ _____ which can build up in your muscles and cause cramp. To break

down the acid, you have to breathe in extra oxygen. This is called an _____ _____.

Microorganisms such as yeast carry out a type of anaerobic respiration called _____. In this reaction,

carbon dioxide and _____ are produced.

B Write down the word equation for anaerobic respiration in animal cells.

_____ → _____

C a Write down the word equation for anaerobic respiration in plant cells.

_____ → _____ + _____ _____

b Name another type of organism that performs fermentation.

_____

D The table shows some statements about respiration.
Tick **one** column in each row to show which statements are true for each type of respiration.

	✓ if true for aerobic respiration	✓ if true for anaerobic respiration
Glucose is a reactant		
Oxygen is a reactant		
Carbon dioxide is produced		
Lactic acid is produced		
Water is produced		

E a Give **two** reasons why animals normally carry out aerobic respiration.

1 _____

2 _____

b Give **one** reason why animals respire anaerobically.

_____

9.3.3 Biotechnology

A Fill in the gaps to complete the sentences.

The microorganism _____ is used to make bread and alcoholic drinks such as _____

and wine. During _____, glucose is converted into carbon dioxide and _____.

_____ in yeast speed up this process making the reaction occur _____.

B Complete the word equation for fermentation.

Choose from the following words:

ethanol	oxygen	lactic acid	glucose	water

_____ → _____ + carbon dioxide

C The statements below can be reordered to describe how beer and wine are made.
Read the statements and write down the order that you think will give the best description.

Correct order: ☐ ☐ ☐ ☐ ☐

1 The liquid is put into bottles or barrels.

2 The mixture is left until all the sugar has fermented.

3 Yeast is added to plant sugar in a large container.

4 The yeast ferments the sugar into alcohol.

5 The liquid is filtered to remove any sediment.

D Explain why bread does not contain alcohol.

_____

_____

E Describe the optimum conditions for bread production.

_____

F Explain how temperature affects the rate of fermentation.

_____

_____

_____

_____

9.4.1 Photosynthesis

A Fill in the gaps to complete the sentences.

Plants and _____ are called _____ because they make their own food by the process

of _____. Animals are called _____ as they have to eat other organisms to survive.

During photosynthesis, carbon dioxide and _____ are converted into oxygen and _____

using energy from the Sun. This light energy is absorbed by _____ in chloroplasts.

B Plants and algae both produce their own food by the process of photosynthesis.

   a Complete the word equation for photosynthesis.

carbon dioxide + _____ $\xrightarrow{\hspace{3cm}}$ glucose + _____

   b Circle the products of photosynthesis.

   c Underline the reactants of photosynthesis.

C Describe how the following enter a plant to be used in photosynthesis.

   a Carbon dioxide _____

   b Water _____

   c Light _____

D **a** Explain how plants are adapted to provide water for photosynthesis.

_____

_____

_____

   b Explain why plants need to continually take in water from the soil.

_____

_____

_____

E Explain why photosynthesis is important for all organisms in a food chain.

_____

_____

_____

9.4.2 Leaves

A Fill in the gaps to complete the sentences.

Photosynthesis in a plant mainly takes place in the _____, though a small amount occurs in the stems.

The underneath of a leaf contains tiny holes called _____ which allow _____ _____ to

diffuse into the leaf and _____ to diffuse out. Water is carried to the leaf in the _____.

Most photosynthesis occurs in the cells of the _____ layer as most light reaches this layer. Therefore,

these cells are full of _____.

B Label the diagram of the cross-section through a leaf.

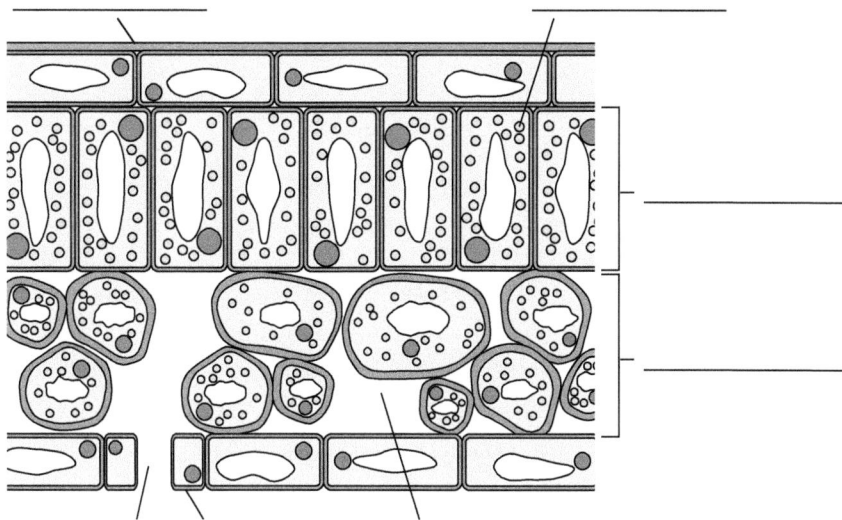

C Describe the function of the following parts of a leaf.

a Veins _____

b Waxy layer _____

c Guard cells _____

d Stomata _____

D Explain the distribution of chloroplasts in a leaf and their role in photosynthesis.

_____

_____

_____

E Explain why most leaves are thin and have a large surface area.

_____

_____

_____

9.4.3 Investigating photosynthesis

A Fill in the gaps to complete the sentences.

You can test a leaf for starch by adding a few drops of _____ . It will change from yellow-orange to

_____ - _____ . You can measure how fast a plant is photosynthesising by counting

the number of bubbles of _____ given off in a fixed time.

The main factors which affect the rate of photosynthesis are _____ intensity, _____

_____ concentration, and _____ . In general, increasing each of these factors

_____ the rate of photosynthesis.

B **a** The statements below can be reordered to describe how to test a leaf for the presence of starch.
Read the statements and write down the order that you think will give the best description.

Correct order: ☐ ☐ ☐ ☐ ☐

1 Add a few drops of iodine solution.

2 Iodine will turn blue-black if starch is present.

3 Wash leaf and place on white tile.

4 Place leaf in boiling water.

5 Place in boiling ethanol to remove chlorophyll.

b The leaf tested had a white striped pattern. Explain why the white areas of the leaf stayed a yellow-brown colour after testing.

_____

_____

_____

C In the space below, sketch and annotate a graph to describe the relationship between temperature and the rate of photosynthesis.

D Explain **one** method that could be used to investigate the rate of photosynthesis.

_____

_____

_____

9.4.4 Plant minerals

A Fill in the gaps to complete the sentences.

To stay healthy, plants need to absorb _____ from the soil. For healthy growth, plants need

four minerals – _____ to make chlorophyll, _____ for healthy leaves and flowers,

_____ for healthy growth and _____ for healthy roots. If a plant does not get enough

of a mineral it is said to have a _____ and will not grow properly. To prevent this occurring, farmers

add chemicals called _____ to the soil.

B Draw a line to match each mineral to its use in the plant, and describe the plant's appearance if this mineral
is deficient.

Mineral	Function	Deficiency symptoms
Nitrate	Making chlorophyll	
Phosphate	Healthy growth	
Potassium	Healthy roots	
Magnesium	Healthy leaves and flowers	

C Deficiency in the mineral potassium can result in yellow leaves.

a Name one other mineral deficiency that results in yellow leaves.

_____

b Explain how the deficiency results in yellow leaves.

_____

_____

D A scientist measured the height of a number of tomato plant seedlings after a month of growth. Each received the
same amount of water and light but received different types of mineral supplement.

Three mineral supplements were tested, labelled A, B, and C. One sample contained nitrogen, phosphorus, and
magnesium; one sample contained nitrogen and magnesium; and one sample contained no useful minerals. Five
seedlings were placed in each supplement.

a The height of seedlings grown using supplement A was measured. The results are shown below.

24.6 cm   32.5 cm   31.5 cm   34.0 cm   32.4 cm

Calculate the mean height of these seedlings.

_____

b The mean height of seedlings grown in supplement B was 20.4 cm, and in supplement C was 21.2 cm.

Is there enough evidence to work out which plant received a 'dummy' supplement, containing no useful
minerals? Explain your answer.

_____

_____

Big Idea 9 Pinchpoint ⧖

Pinchpoint question

Answer the question below, then do the follow-up activity **with the same letter** as the answer you picked.

Which of the following statements best describes the process of photosynthesis?

A Can be represented by the word equation glucose + oxygen → carbon dioxide + water

B The method by which plants inhale carbon dioxide and exhale oxygen

C The process by which plants use water and minerals from the soil to make glucose

D The production of glucose and oxygen from carbon dioxide and water

Follow-up activities

A The following paragraph describes what happens in photosynthesis. Read the paragraph then complete the activities listed below.

Plants make food by the process of photosynthesis. Photosynthesis is a chemical reaction in which plants take in carbon dioxide and water and convert them into glucose. This provides the plant with food. Oxygen is also produced, which is released back into the atmosphere. This is used by plants and animals in respiration.

a Underline the **two** reactants of photosynthesis.

b Circle the **two** products of photosynthesis.

c Complete the word equation for photosynthesis.

_____ + _____ ⎯⎯⎯⎯⟶ _____ + _____

Hint: Reactants are the starting substances in a chemical reaction. For help, see 9.4.1 Photosynthesis.

B Circle the correct **bold** terms in the sentences below to describe how plants exchange gases, and their uses in the plant.

Plants take in air containing oxygen and carbon dioxide through their **lungs / leaves**. The gases diffuse into the

plant through tiny pores called **stomata / alveoli**.

Both carbon dioxide and oxygen are used for different processes inside the plant. Photosynthesis requires

carbon dioxide / oxygen, while **carbon dioxide / oxygen** is needed for respiration.

Plants do release some oxygen from their leaves as it is produced as a result of **respiration / photosynthesis**.

However, it is not released through breathing. It passes out of the leaf through the **stomata / alveoli**, again

through the process of diffusion. Some of the oxygen remains in the plant and is used in respiration to produce

glucose / energy.

Hint: Think about the structure of a leaf. How is it adapted for gas exchange? For help, see 9.4.1 Photosynthesis and 9.4.4 Leaves.

C A group of students grew some seedlings in petri dishes on a warm window sill. The table below shows their observations after four weeks.

Dish	Conditions	Observations
1	Seedling roots placed into cotton wool ball	Shrivelled appearance, dead
2	Seedling roots placed into cotton wool ball soaked in distilled (pure) water. Water replaced every two days.	Shoots with leaves, some spindly and some yellow, plant alive and growing
3	Seedling roots placed into dry, mineral rich soil	Shrivelled appearance, dead
4	Seedling roots placed into mineral rich soil and distilled water. Water replaced every two days.	Green shoots and leaves, plant alive and growing

a Name the dish where the plants grew best. _____

b Explain the observations gained by the group of students.

_____

_____

_____

Hint: What reactants are needed for photosynthesis? For help, see 9.4.1 Photosynthesis and 9.4.4 Plant minerals.

D A group of students investigated how light intensity affected the rate of photosynthesis. Their results are shown on the graph below.

a Describe the trend shown by the graph.

_____

_____

_____

b At a relative light intensity of 0, the relative rate of photosynthesis was also 0. Explain why.

_____

_____

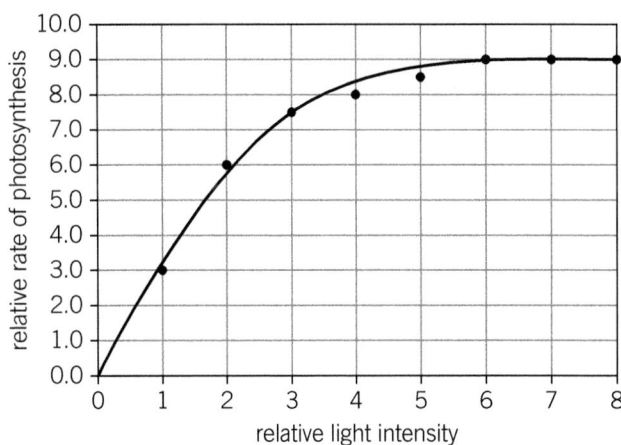

c Suggest and explain the relative rate of photosynthesis at a relative light intensity of 10.

_____

_____

Hint: Think about the word equation for photosynthesis. To maximise the rate of photosynthesis you need to maximise the availability of the reactants. For help, see 9.4.3 Investigating photosynthesis.

⊗ Pinchpoint review

Now look back at the question – do you think you chose the right letter?
Turn to the Answers page to find out.

10.3.1 Natural selection

A Fill in the gaps to complete the sentences.

All organisms living today have _____ from a common ancestor. This process has taken

_____ of years and has occurred as a result of _____ _____.

The organisms most adapted to their environment _____ and reproduce, passing on the

_____ which code for these characteristics to their offspring. The remains of organisms that lived

millions of years ago, called _____, provide evidence for evolution.

B The statements below can be reordered to describe how a species evolves through the process of natural selection. Read the statements and write down the order of statements you think will give the best description.

Correct order: ☐ ☐ ☐ ☐ ☐ ☐

1 Process is repeated over many generations.
2 Genes which code for advantageous characteristics are passed on to offspring.
3 New species can evolve where all organisms have the adaptations.
4 Organisms in a species show variation.
5 More organisms within the species have the advantageous characteristic.
6 The organisms with the characteristics that are best suited to the environment survive and reproduce. Less well-adapted organisms die.

C Fossils provide important evidence for evolution.

a Describe what a fossil is.

_____

b Explain how fossils provide evidence for evolution.

_____

D Using a named example, explain how natural selection leads to evolution.

_____

_____

_____

_____

10.3.2 Charles Darwin

A Fill in the gaps to complete the sentences.

Charles _____'s theory states that organisms _____ as a result of natural _____. He noticed that finches on different islands in the Galapagos had different _____ and claws.

These were linked to the type of food available. He concluded that if a bird was born with a beak suited to the food available it would survive and _____. Over time, all the birds on this island would have this characteristic.

Before he published this theory, it was _____ reviewed by a fellow scientist called Alfred _____.

B Before scientists publish their work in a scientific journal, it is peer-reviewed.

Describe what is meant by peer review.

_____

_____

_____

C Draw a line to match each piece of evidence with how it supports Darwin's theory of natural selection.

Fossil record	Micro-organisms best suited for their environment survive and reproduce
Extinction	Organisms have changed over time (millions of years)
Development of antibiotic-resistant bacteria	Species that do not adapt to environmental changes die out

D Darwin studied finches living on different islands in the Galapagos.

Explain how Darwin used this evidence to develop his theory of natural selection and evolution.

_____

_____

_____

_____

_____

_____

Hint: First describe the evidence Darwin collected. Then explain how he used it to develop his theory.

10.3.3 Extinction

A Fill in the gaps to complete the sentences.

The range of organisms living in an area is called _____. Destruction of _____ and

outbreaks of _____ can cause a reduction in biodiversity and can lead to a species becoming

_____. This is where there are no individuals of a species living anywhere in the world. When only a

small number of a species exist, the species is said to be _____.

B **a** Name an example of an area of high biodiversity. _____

   b Name an example of an area of low biodiversity. _____

   c Explain why the loss of a plant species from an area will have a greater effect in an area of low biodiversity than in an area of high biodiversity.

_____

_____

_____

_____

C Explain **three** factors that could lead to a species becoming extinct.

   1 _____

_____

   2 _____

_____

   3 _____

_____

10.3.4 Preserving biodiversity

A Fill in the gaps to complete the sentences.

Species that are at risk of becoming extinct are said to be _____. Scientists use a number of

techniques to prevent this occurring. This includes protecting habitats through _____,

the _____ breeding of animals, and storing genetic samples in gene _____.

Preserving biodiversity not only ensures that a species _____ but can provide useful resources

for other organisms, including humans.

B Draw a line to match each method of preventing extinction with its description and how it works.

| Conservation | Breeding animals in human-controlled environments | Material can be used for research or in some cases used to create new individuals |

| Captive breeding | Store genetic samples such as seeds at very low temperatures | Creates a healthy stable population that can be reintroduced back into the wild |

| Gene banks | Protecting a natural environment | Increases organisms' chance of survival and reduces disruption to food chains |

C Bengal tigers are an example of an endangered population.

   a Describe **two** advantages of captive breeding of Bengal tigers.

     1 _____

     2 _____

   b Describe **two** disadvantages of captive breeding of Bengal tigers.

     1 _____

     2 _____

D Suggest and explain **one** other technique that could be used to prevent Bengal tigers becoming extinct.

_____

_____

_____

10.4.1 Inheritance

A Fill in the gaps to complete the sentences.

You inherit characteristics from your parents through genetic material found in the _____ of your

cells. Genetic material is made up of the chemical _____ – this contains all the information needed

to make an organism. In the nucleus, this chemical is organised into long strands called _____.

Each strand is divided into sections called _____. Each section contains the information needed to

produce a characteristic.

B Annotate the diagram to explain how characteristics are passed on from parents to their offspring.
Use the following terms:

| sperm | egg | nucleus | chromosome | 23 | 46 |

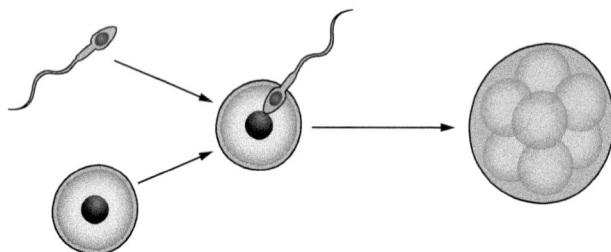

C Explain the function of a gene.

_____

_____

D a Describe what is meant by a mutation.

_____

b Explain how a mutation can be passed on to an organism's offspring.

_____

_____

10.4.2 DNA

A Fill in the gaps to complete the sentences.

Your DNA is found in the _____ of your cells. It is made of _____ strands. These are twisted together to form a double _____. The strands are held together by four different

_____.

The structure of DNA was discovered by four scientists. Wilkins and _____ took a picture of DNA using _____. _____ and Crick looked at this image and identified that the structure of DNA was a _____ shape.

B Describe **three** features of the structure of DNA.

1 _____

2 _____

3 _____

C Choose from the words below to fill in the blanks in the sentences.

sharing	pea	helix	structure	working
nucleus	discoveries	DNA	characteristics	

The earliest work on how _____ are inherited was completed by Gregor Mendel, in 1866.

He experimented on _____ plants. A few years later, Friedrich Meischer discovered an acidic

substance in the _____ of cells. We now call this substance DNA.

By the early 1950s, Maurice Wilkins and Rosalind Franklin used X-rays to photograph crystals of _____.

This work enabled James Watson and Francis Crick to work out the _____ of the DNA molecule.

They deduced it has a double _____ shape.

The discovery of the structure of DNA is the result of many scientists _____ together, through

_____ their results. This is the way many scientific _____ are made.

D Explain **two** reasons why it is important for scientists to work together.

1 _____

_____

2 _____

_____

10.4.3 Genetics

A Fill in the gaps to complete the sentences.

Different forms of the same gene are called _____. If a _____ allele is present it will

always be expressed. A _____ allele will only be expressed if two copies of the allele are present.

A _____ square can be used to predict the outcomes of a genetic cross.

B In humans, the allele for freckles is dominant. It can be represented using the letter F. The allele for no freckles is recessive and can be represented by the letter f.

Give the characteristic that will be displayed in a person with the following allele combinations.

FF _____   Ff_____   ff_____

C In mice, the allele for black fur is dominant (B) and the allele for white fur is recessive (b).

   a Use the following Punnett square to show the likelihood of a mouse having black fur. In this example, the female mouse carries alleles BB; the male mouse carries alleles bb.

Female

Male		

_____ of the offspring will have black fur

   b Draw a Punnett square to show what would happen if you cross two mice with the alleles Bb.

_____% of mice will have black fur

_____% of mice will have white fur

D In humans, having dimples is a dominant characteristic.

Explain how a mother and father who both have dimples can produce offspring without dimples.

_____

_____

_____

Hint: You can use a Punnett square in your answer.

10.4.4 Genetic modification

A Fill in the gaps to complete the sentences.

Scientists can create an organism with desired _____ by taking _____ from another organism. These are called _____ genes. They are placed into plant or animal _____ at a very early stage in development. As the organism develops it will now display the desired characteristics.

B Reorder the statements below to describe how an organism can be genetically modified.

Correct order: ☐ ☐ ☐ ☐

1 Take genes from an organism with that characteristic.

2 As the organism develops, it will display the characteristics of the foreign genes.

3 Identify the desired characteristic such as frost-resistance.

4 Place them into an organism at a very early stage of development.

C Describe **two** advantages of producing products through genetic modification.

1 _____

2 _____

D Some people have concerns over genetically modifying organisms.

Explain **two** possible disadvantages of genetically modifying crops.

1 _____

_____

2 _____

_____

Big Idea 10 Pinchpoint ⊗

Pinchpoint question

Answer the question below, then do the follow-up activity **with the same letter** as the answer you picked.

Which of the following statements best describes the process of evolution by natural selection?

A Process by which an organism with an advantageous adaptation survives and passes on the characteristic. The entire next generation are adapted and have the beneficial characteristic.

B Process by which a species changes over many generations to become better adapted to its environment.

C Evolution involves changes to a species. This process always takes millions of years.

D Process by which an organism changes to become better suited to its environment.

Follow-up activities

A In an area of land, there are 15 000 organisms of species X, a predator. For species X, the faster the organism the more chance it has of survival, as it is more able to catch its prey.

The table below shows how the species evolves over time to become faster. The overall population of species X remains constant.

Generation	1	2	5	10	100
Number of individuals who can run at over 40 km/h	75	150	500	1000	5000

a Calculate the proportion of offspring in the original generation that can run faster than 40 km/h. _____

b Calculate the proportion of offspring in generation 100 that can run faster than 40 km/h. _____

c Explain the difference in your answers to parts **a** and **b**.

_____

_____

_____

Hint: To calculate a percentage, divide the number in the generation by the total population. To help you explain in part **c**, see 10.3.1 Natural selection.

B Pathogens such as bacteria and viruses reproduce very rapidly and can evolve in a relatively short time. Explain how the evolution of bacteria can lead to antibiotic resistance.

_____

_____

_____

_____

_____

Hint: Due to variation, some bacteria in a species may be naturally resistant to an antibiotic. For help, see 10.3.1 Natural Selection.

C a Choose the appropriate words from the list below to complete the following sentences which describe how peppered moths evolved. You will need to use some words more than once

camouflaged	pale	increasing	eaten	dark	reproduced	soot	decreasing

There are two types of peppered moth: pale moths and dark moths. Before the industrial revolution there

were more _____ moths as these were _____ against the pale tree bark;

_____ moths were seen and _____. More _____ moths survived

and _____ increasing the number of these moths in the population.

After the industrial revolution, many trees in urban areas were covered in _____. The

_____ moths were now more _____ so survived and reproduced. This resulted

in the number of pale moths _____, and the number of dark moths _____. Most

moths in the population were now _____.

b The first dark peppered moth was recorded in Manchester in 1848. By 1895, 98% of peppered moths in the city were black. Calculate the number of years over which this example of evolution took place.

_____.

Hint: In order to pass on a characteristic an organism needs to survive and reproduce. For help, see 10.3.1 Natural selection.

D The statements below describe how the giraffe species has evolved over time to have longer necks. Add a picture in the box next to each statement to show what is occurring.

1	2	3

Originally there were short- and long-necked giraffes within the population

Long-necked giraffes had an advantage as they could reach the taller trees

More long-necked giraffes survived. Short-necked giraffes died due to a lack of food

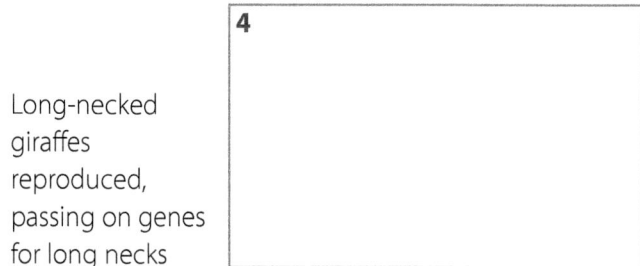

4	5

Long-necked giraffes reproduced, passing on genes for long necks

After many generations, all giraffes have long necks

Hint: Include images of several giraffes in your pictures, as evolution applies to a species, not an individual organism. For help, see 10.3.1 Natural selection.

⊃⊂ **Pinchpoint review**

Now look back at the question – do you think you chose the right letter?
Turn to the Answers page to find out.

Section 3 Revision questions

1 🧪🧪 Woolly mammoths are an example of a species that is extinct.

a i Explain what is meant by the term 'extinct'. *(1 mark)*

_____

_____

ii Suggest **one** reason why woolly mammoths became extinct. *(1 mark)*

_____

b Describe how the extinction of a species affects the biodiversity in an ecosystem. *(2 marks)*

_____

_____

_____

2 🧪🧪 A group of students were investigating the types of nutrient present in different ready meals.

a Draw a line to match each nutrient to its role in the body. *(2 marks)*

Protein		Main source of energy

Lipids		To provide a store of energy and insulation, and protect organs

Carbohydrates		To repair body tissues and make new cells

b The ready meals also contained fibre. Explain the importance of fibre in a person's diet. *(2 marks)*

_____

_____

_____

c One of the ready meals stated that it contained 2520 kJ of energy per pack. An average adult requires 8400 kJ of energy per day. Calculate the percentage of an adult's daily energy requirement contained within this pack. *(2 marks)*

_____ kJ

d Describe how the students could prove that sugar was present in one of the ready meals *(3 marks)*

_____

_____

_____

_____

3 🧪🧪 Digestion begins in your mouth when food is chewed and mixed with saliva.

a i Name the enzyme present in saliva. *(1 mark)*

_____

ii Describe the role of this enzyme in digestion. *(2 marks)*

_____

_____

_____

b Explain why enzymes are called biological catalysts. *(2 marks)*

_____

_____

_____

c Bacteria that live in your large intestine play an important role in digestion. Describe the role these bacteria play. *(2 marks)*

_____

_____

_____

4 🧪🧪 You get energy from the food you eat. This energy is transferred to your cells by respiration.

a i Complete the word equation for aerobic respiration. *(2 marks)*

glucose + _____ →
carbon dioxide + _____

ii Write down where in the cell respiration takes place. *(1 mark)*

_____

b Write down **two** differences between aerobic and anaerobic respiration in humans. *(2 marks)*

_____

_____

_____

_____

c **i** Write down what type of respiration is being represented by the following word equation:

glucose → ethanol + carbon dioxide (+ energy)

(1 mark)

_____

ii Name an organism that performs this type of respiration. *(1 mark)*

_____

5 ⚗️⚗️**Figure 1** shows a structure found in your lungs.

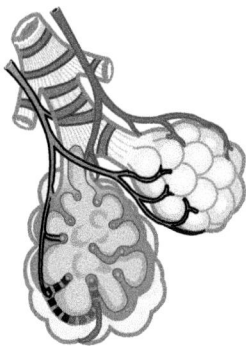

Figure 1

a Name the structure that forms the gas exchange surface. *(1 mark)*

_____

b Describe this structure's role in gas exchange. *(2 marks)*

_____

_____

c Explain how this structure is adapted to perform its function. *(3 marks)*

_____

_____

_____

6 ⚗️⚗️ A student measured his lung volume using the equipment shown in **Figure 2**.

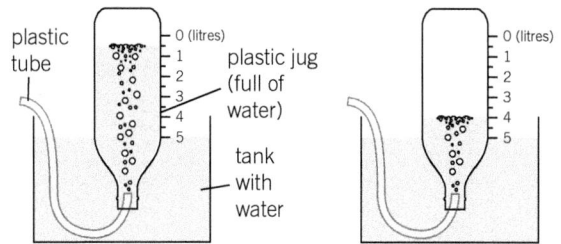

Figure 2

a Calculate the volume of air exhaled by the student. *(2 marks)*

_____

_____ litres

b Write down **two** differences between the air exhaled by the student, and the air inhaled. *(2 marks)*

1 _____

2 _____

c Suggest **one** factor that could reduce the student's lung volume. *(1 mark)*

_____

7 ⚗️⚗️ In the 19th century, Charles Darwin developed the theory of evolution.

a **i** Name the process through which organisms evolve over time. *(1 mark)*

_____

ii Describe **one** piece of evidence Darwin used to develop the theory of evolution. *(2 marks)*

_____

_____

b Darwin and a second scientist, Alfred Wallace, were working on similar theories at the same time. Darwin and Wallace peer-reviewed each other's work.

Describe what is meant by the term 'peer review'. *(2 marks)*

_____

_____

_____

8 🔬🔬 The graph shows the number of people who died due to different diseases caused by smoking.

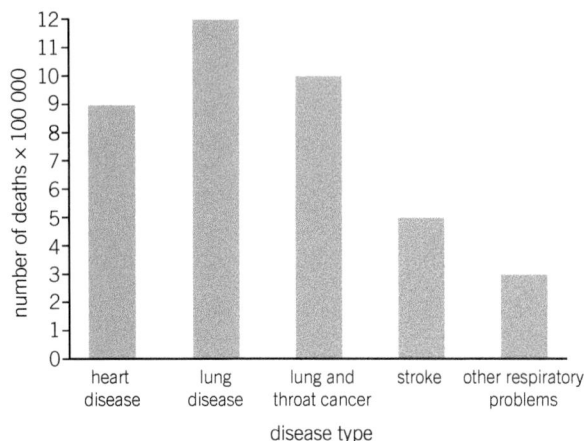

a Name the addictive drug in tobacco smoke.
(1 mark)

_____

b How many people died due to lung disease?
(1 mark)

_____

c Which disease type caused twice as many deaths as strokes? *(1 mark)*

_____

d Explain why smoking increases the risk of suffering from a respiratory infection. *(4 marks)*

_____

_____

_____

_____

9 🔬🔬 Plants and animals compete for resources to survive.

A new predator is introduced into an area. Describe how its prey species could change over a long period of time to survive a new predator. *(6 marks)*

_____

_____

_____

_____

_____

_____

_____

10 🔬🔬 **a** Describe the difference between a dominant and a recessive allele. *(2 marks)*

_____

_____

_____

b In pea plants, purple flowers are dominant (P) and white flowers are recessive (p). A plant with the alleles Pp was crossed with another plant with the alleles pp.

Complete the following Punnett square to calculate the likelihood of one of the offspring having white flowers. *(3 marks)*

		Plant 1	
		P	p
Plant 2	P		
	p		

_____

11 🔬🔬 **a** Describe how an organism can be genetically modified. *(3 marks)*

_____

_____

_____

_____

b Describe **two** advantages of producing products through genetic modification. *(4 marks)*

1 _____

_____

2 _____

_____

12 🔬🔬🔬 Drugs are chemicals that affect the way the body works.

a Describe the difference between a recreational and a medical drug. *(2 marks)*

_____

_____

_____

b i Name the drug found in wine and beer.
(1 mark)

_____

ii Give the long-term effects on the body of the drug identified in part **i**. *(3 marks)*

_____

_____

_____

_____

c Smoking tobacco increases your risk of developing cardiovascular disease (CVD). This includes heart attacks and strokes.

i Explain how smoking can lead to heart disease. *(1 mark)*

_____

_____

_____

ii Study **Table 1.**

Table 1

Cigarettes smoked per day	CVD deaths per 100 000 men per year
0	572
1–14	802
15–24	892
25+	1025

Calculate the increase in the number of deaths due to CVD between men who smokes 20 cigarettes a day, compared to a non-smoker. *(1 mark)*

_____ per 100 000 men per year

iii Calculate the percentage of men dying from CVD each year who smoke 25 or more cigarettes per day. *(2 marks)*

_____ per 100 000 men per year

13 🏺🏺🏺 A breeder of rabbits crossed a rabbit with brown spots with a rabbit with no spots.

a Explain why some of the rabbits had brown spots but some had no spots. *(1 mark)*

_____

_____

b An adult rabbit has 44 chromosomes in its body cells. How many chromosomes are present in:

i a sperm cell? _____ *(1 mark)*

ii a fertilised egg cell? _____ *(1 mark)*

14 🏺🏺🏺 A group of students tested a variegated leaf for the presence of starch.

a Describe how to test a leaf for the presence of starch. *(3 marks)*

_____

_____

_____

_____

b **i** Shade in **Figure 3** below to show the results you would expect the students to see. *(1 mark)*

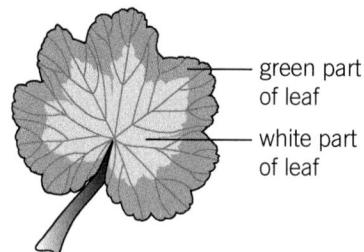

green part of leaf

white part of leaf

Figure 3

ii Explain your answer to part **i**. *(4 marks)*

_____

_____

_____

_____

15 🏺🏺🏺 All organisms contain genetic material.

a Explain how genetic material is organised inside a cell. *(4 marks)*

_____

_____

_____

_____

b Explain how the structure of DNA was discovered. *(4 marks)*

_____

_____

_____

_____

Section 3 Checklist

Revision question number	Outcome	Topic reference	😞	😐	😊
1	State what is meant by the term extinct. State what is meant by biodiversity.	10.3.3			
2a, b	Explain the role of each nutrient in the body.	8.4.1			
2c	Calculate energy requirements.	8.4.3 🧮			
2d	Describe how to test foods for the presence of sugars.	8.4.2			
3a, b	Describe the role of enzymes in digestion.	8.4.5			
3c	Describe the role of bacteria in digestion.	8.4.5			
4a	State the word equation for aerobic respiration.	9.3.1			
4b, c	Describe the differences between aerobic and anaerobic respiration.	9.3.2			
5a	Name the parts of the gas exchange system.	8.3.1			
5b	Describe the role of the alveoli in gas exchange.	8.3.1			
5c	Describe how the parts of the gas exchange system are adapted to their function.	8.3.1			
6a	Calculate lung volume from the results of an experiment.	8.3.2 🧮			
6b	Describe the differences between inhaled and exhaled air.	8.3.1			
6c	Suggest factors that could affect lung volume.	8.3.2			
7a	Name the process by which organisms evolve.	10.3.2			
7b	Explain the importance of peer review to scientists.	10.3.2			
8a	Describe the effects of tobacco smoke on health.	8.3.5			
8b, c	Interpret secondary data to draw conclusions.	8.3.5			
8d	Explain how smoking causes disease.	8.3.5			
9	Describe the process of natural selection.	10.3.1			
10a	Describe the difference between dominant and recessive alleles.	10.4.3			
10b	Use a Punnett square to show what happens during a genetic cross.	10.4.3			
11a	Describe how an organism can be genetically modified.	10.4.4			
11b	Describe some advantages of producing products through genetic modification.	10.4.4			
12a	Describe the difference between recreational and medicinal drugs.	8.3.3			
12b	Explain in detail how alcohol affects health and behaviour.	8.3.4			
12c	Explain how smoking causes diseases. Interpret secondary data in an appropriate manner, extrapolating data from trends shown.	8.3.5 🧮			
13	Explain how characteristics are inherited.	10.4.1			
14	Carry out an experiment to test for the presence of starch in a leaf, explaining the results obtained.	9.4.3			
15a	Describe the relationship between DNA, genes, and chromosomes.	10.4.1			
15b	Describe how scientists worked together to discover the structure of DNA.	10.4.2			

Answers

EP6

A   data, measurements, independent, dependent, control, repeatable

B   observational enquiry – 2, 5; pattern-seeking enquiry – 1, 6; not a scientific question – 3, 4

C   so you know the independent variable is causing the effect, not another variable

D   **a**   whether breakfast is eaten

   b   number of press-ups completed

   c   e.g. time breakfast eaten, time press-ups completed, person, type of breakfast eaten, mass of breakfast eaten

E   **a**   there is no scientific definition of what best is / people's opinions would be different

   b   **two** appropriate suggestions, e.g. which material can hold the most mass / is the cheapest per unit area / is the most waterproof / is the strongest / is the lowest density

EP7

A   best fit, same, secondary, conclusion.

B   **a**   graph 1

   b   graph 2 – line of best fit too high; graph 3 – line of best fit too low; graph 4 – a line of best fit has not been drawn / student connected the data points 'dot to dot'

C   **two** from: compare your results with other groups who have carried out the same investigation / repeat experiment / compare your results with secondary data

D   **a**   larger range allows you to see if a trend continues for more values of the independent variable; smaller interval allows you to collect more data for the range chosen, so increasing the reliability of the data collected

   b   **two** from: time constraints / cost / equipment not available / measuring instruments not precise enough / other appropriate suggestion

EP8

A   effective, read, audience, purpose

B   a3, b1, c2

C   "height of the step" written twice – not concise; "it was careful" – not clear, what was careful?

D   use technical language for the journal but not the magazine, as scientists in that field will understand that terminology but the audience of the magazine might not; want attention-grabbing content (with illustrations / pictures) for the magazine to interest readers, but not important for the journal as scientists need to read it anyway

EP9

A   evidence, peer review, journal, funder, bias

B   peer review involves scientists who are experts in the same field checking whether the work is correct, making it less likely it is inaccurate or includes a mistake

C   a1, b3, c2

D   experimentation, deny, guarantee, reporting, requires, never

EP10

A   true, evidence, observations, argument, evidence

B   **a**   there are dunes of frozen methane on Pluto

   b   a photo of Pluto shows wavy ridges, similar to satellite images of the sand dunes of the Sahara Desert

   c   winds on Pluto are not strong enough to lift methane grains off the surface

   d   any suitable opinion, e.g. *I think the evidence in part b is stronger*

   e   e.g. it is easy to see from the image that the wavy ridges on the photo of Pluto are similar to satellite images of the sand dunes of the Sahara desert, but it is more difficult to be certain that the winds on Pluto are not strong enough to lift methane grains off the ground

   f   e.g. get some solid nitrogen, and place some grains of solid methane on top of it; warm the solid nitrogen, or reduce the pressure, to make the solid nitrogen sublime; observe whether the grains of methane are lifted into the air

EP11

A   benefits, different, risks

B   e.g. top line – increased exercise / fitness, become obsessed with number of steps; bottom line – people might walk instead of using polluting cars to increase number of steps, more electronic waste / large amounts of resources used to make fitness trackers

C   **a**   e.g. encourages daughter to exercise

   b   e.g. distraction to learning

   c   e.g. profit increases

D   **a**   possible side-effects, e.g. sore arms / getting flu but less badly

   b   e.g. less likely to get flu, fewer people require expensive hospital stays

   c   any suitable justification – must include the point that benefits outweigh risks

EP12

A   explanation, evidence, kinetic, Big Bang, evidence

B   **a**   2, 4, 5, 6, 8

   b   1 – **All** scientific theories are supported by evidence. 3 – Scientific theories **may change** over time. 7 – Scientists **can** use theories to make predictions.

C   **a**   kinetic, Big Bang, germ

   b   e.g. pumping more air into a tyre increases the pressure inside the tyre; the Universe will continue to expand / stars and galaxies will get further apart; if a student has a cold, many others at the same school will also get colds

D   a model represents something that is too difficult to display, usually because it is too big, too small or too complicated; it does not explain anything; a theory is an explanation for patterns in observations or data, and must be supported by evidence; theories can be used to make predictions

EP13

A   theory, new, evidence, conferences, correct, tested, correct, argumentation

B   reason to change a theory – a, b, d, f; longer to accept a new theory – c, e

C   **a**   trying to find out why it may be wrong / testing the predictions it makes

   b   there are data or observations that do not support it

   c   the new theory is stronger than it would otherwise be

D   **a**   using logical reasoning, debate, and negotiation to reach conclusions

   b   to ensure that theories are robust / as strong as possible

   c   incorrect theories might be introduced; scientists could publish what they like without being challenged

Enquiry Processes Pinchpoint

A   this is an incorrect answer – scientists change their mind when **new evidence is found**

B   this is an incorrect answer – scientific laws **describe** phenomena, while scientific theories **explain** them

C   this is the correct answer

D   this is an incorrect answer – scientists base their theories on **scientific evidence and peer review**

Pinchpoint follow-up

A germ theory, evidence, bacteria, heat, diseases, evidence, theory, evidence, antibiotic, evidence, theory

B a2, b1, c3

C discovery of antibiotics; discovery of DNA; splitting the atom; Hubble telescope

D 1, 3, 5, 6, 7, 8

1.3.1

A friction, rough, lubrication, air, water (either order), streamlined, slow down, contact, resultant, equilibrium, stationary, same, direction, newton

B
  a weight (gravity)
  b air resistance (drag due to air)
  c continue moving with same speed in the same direction

C
  a boat slows down / stops / speed decreases; drag (or water resistance) pushes on boat opposite to the direction of its motion; no other force acting horizontally after engine stops, unbalanced force; have to push water molecules (or particles) out of the way to move forward
  b box slows down / stops / speed decreases; friction pushes on box opposite to direction of its motion; no other force acting horizontally after person stops pushing, unbalanced force; surface of floor is rough when look on small enough scale

1.3.2

A deform, compress, pushes, reaction, stretch, extension, tension, double, Hooke's Law, proportional, elastic, linear, linear, origin

B $\frac{200}{50} = 4$; $1.2 \times 4 = 4.8\,\text{cm}$

C strap – stretch; weight of bag pulls down, support from person pulls up; tyre – compress; weight of person (bike / wheel rim) pushes down, support force from road pushes up

D the Earth pulls down on you with a force of gravity, your weight; your weight pushes the particles in the floor together; the bonds between the particles in the floor are compressed; the bonds push back and support you

1.3.3

A pivot, moment, moment, force, distance, pivot, newton metre, force, pivot, moment, equilibrium, law of moments, weight, above, below (either order), no, topple

B
  a moment (Nm) = force (N) × perpendicular distance from the pivot (m)
  b $5.0 \times 0.50 = 2.5\,\text{N m}$
  c $50 \times 0.40 = 20\,\text{N m}$
  d so there is no turning moment due to their weight, so they do not topple off the rope

C
  a $\text{force} = \frac{\text{moment}}{\text{distance}}$
  b i $\text{force} = \frac{10\,\text{N m}}{0.110\,\text{m}} = 91\,\text{N}$
    ii yes, as the force required is less than the force she can exert

1.4.1

A fluid, gas pressure, particles, compressed, density, force, area, newtons per square metre, force, pressure, atmospheric pressure, atmospheric pressure, smaller / less

B pressure decreases with height; less oxygen so harder to breathe / can cause altitude sickness

C you can kick a football further because air particles collide with objects less often so there is less drag; athletes cannot run as far or as fast because there is less oxygen per litre; the speed of sound is lower because neighbouring air particles collide with each other less often

D
  a $\text{pressure} = \frac{\text{force}}{\text{area}}$
  b $\text{pressure} = \frac{\text{force}}{\text{area}}$, so force = pressure × area = $100\,000 \times 0.020$
    $= 2000\,\text{N}$

1.4.2

A liquid pressure, pressure, upthrust, density, incompressible

B
  a upwards arrow from where ship touches water labelled upthrust (or buoyancy); downwards arrow from same place, same length, labelled weight (or gravity)
  b upwards short arrow from middle of anchor labelled upthrust (or buoyancy); downwards long arrow from same place labelled weight (or gravity)

C as you go deeper in the ocean, pressure increases; as you go deeper, there is more weight of water above you, so since pressure = force/ area, the pressure must get larger

D
  a i $\text{pressure} = \frac{\text{force}}{\text{area}}$
    ii $\text{pressure} = \frac{40}{0.40} = 100\,\text{N/m}^2$
  b $\text{pressure} = \frac{\text{force}}{\text{area}}$, so force = pressure × area = $100 \times 4.0 = 400\,\text{N}$

1.4.3

A force, surface area, newtons per square metre, force, stress, large, less

B
  a $\text{stress (N/m}^2) = \frac{\text{force (N)}}{\text{area (m}^2)}$
    $\frac{5.0}{0.010} = 500\,\text{N/m}^2$
  b $\frac{2500}{6.4} = 390\,\text{N/m}^2$ (to 2 sig. fig.)

C
  a weight = mass × gravitational field strength
    $= 78 \times 10 = 780\,\text{N}$
  b $\text{area} = \frac{\text{force}}{\text{pressure}} = \frac{780\,\text{N}}{2800\,\text{N m}^2} = 0.28\,\text{m}^2$

D
  a large paws on lynx mean lower stress on ground, so less likely to sink into snow, making it easier to move around; this is less important to the bobcat because it rarely lives with snow
  b sharp means small area, so large stress to push into the surface; large head means small stress so you do not hurt your thumb

Big Idea 1 Pinchpoint

A this is the correct answer

B this is an incorrect answer – **all types** of object push back on their surroundings with an equal and opposite force

C this is an incorrect answer – the floor pushes up with a **contact reaction force**, not gravity

D this is an incorrect answer – the question asked about the forces on the **chair**, not those on the floor

Pinchpoint follow-up

A
  a cable stretches; the load pulls one end of the cable down, and the crane pulls the other end of the cable up; the particles in the cable are pulled further apart, stretching the bonds in between them; they then pull back towards each other

b force that causes $1.0\,\text{cm} = \dfrac{3.0}{2.0} = 1.5\,\text{kN}$, so force that causes $5.0\,\text{cm} = 1.5 \times 5.0 = 7.5\,\text{kN}\ (7500\,\text{N})$

B **a** 2 (1 is incorrect because the mass must be in a gravitational field; 3 is incorrect because weight acts whether or not a person is pushing)

 b remains stationary

 c vertical arrow from middle of building pointing down labelled weight (gravity); vertical arrow same length pointing up from middle of where building touches ground, labelled reaction or support

C **a** weight – non-contact, mass near Earth; reaction – contact, pushed

 b vertical arrow from middle of building pointing down labelled weight (gravity); vertical arrow same length pointing up from middle of where building touches ground, labelled reaction or support

D **a** force on ground – vertical arrow downwards from middle of where building touches ground; force on building – vertical arrow upwards (**same size**) from middle of where building touches ground

 b bonds, particles, compressed, push, equal, opposite, ground, building, bonds, particles, ground, building

2.3.1

A magnets, magnetic materials, iron, iron, north pole, south pole (either order), north, Earth's, south, different / opposite, same, magnetic field, magnetic field lines, more, force

B **a** attract **b** attract **c** repel **d** repel

C pair of magnets at top of bag need to have different poles facing each other (e.g. N facing a S) because opposite poles attract, closing the bag

D **a**

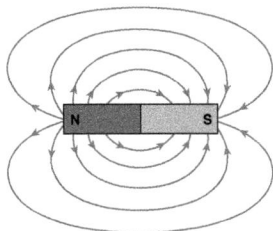

 b S, stronger – near either pole of magnet; W, weaker – far from either pole

E hang / suspend the magnet so that it can spin freely; its north pole will point in the desired direction

2.4.1

A coil, turns / loops, core, more turns, current, material, magnetise, permanent, turned off, field, bar, solenoid

B current, coil, core, magnetic field, current, doesn't

C **two** from: increase number of turns on the coil; increase current flowing in the wire / increase the power supply potential difference; use a magnetic material in the core

D decrease number of turns on coil – weaker – fewer turns adding to field; reverse direction of current – stay the same – just exchanges poles

E yes: any wire carrying current acts as an electromagnet, so both wires act as magnets

2.4.2

A current, coil, iron, bell, iron, current, coil, current, coil, magnet

B 2, 1, 3, 4

C iron bar will pick up magnetic materials when switch is closed, won't pick up non-magnetic ones; need switch so that can drop them into another pile to separate them when switch is opened

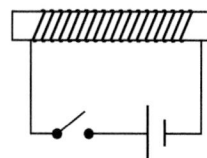

D similarity – **one** from: device triggered by current flowing; current flowing acts as an electromagnet; both use a spring to oppose a magnetic force; both break the circuit
difference – **one** from: bell continues to cause movement as long as current is flowing, but circuit breaker only moves once; circuit breaker breaks circuit only once, but bell continues making and breaking the circuit

E electromagnet, stronger, stronger, lower, more

Big Idea 2 Pinchpoint

A this is an incorrect answer – the current to the speaker **alternates direction** and **varies** in its amount; the current to the bell keeps switching **on and off**

B this is the correct answer

C this is an incorrect answer – the devices depend on **magnetic** forces to move those components

D this is an incorrect answer – the speaker has a **complete** circuit for as long as it is on

Pinchpoint follow-up

A **a** 5, 3, 2, 6, 1, 4

 b there is current in the coil, so it acts as an electromagnet; that causes a magnetic force from the permanent magnet; the varying current causes a varying force, so the diaphragm moves backwards and forwards

B when switch closed, battery supplies a current through the coil; the coil becomes an electromagnet; attracts iron with a magnetic force, large enough to stretch the springs; iron part moves out of the door allowing it to open

C **a** electric – non-contact, charges; magnetic – non-contact, magnetic materials or currents

 b current, electromagnet, magnetic, magnet, magnetic, coil, diaphragm (cone), magnetic, iron, magnetic, armature, breaks

D **a** Current in the coil makes it into **an electromagnet**.

 b The **magnetic** force from the permanent magnet onto the coil depends on the current.

 c The loudspeaker is supplied with a **varying alternating** current all the time the speaker is making a sound.

 d The varying current causes the coil, and therefore the diaphragm (cone), to **move backwards and forwards**.

3.3.1

A work, displacement, energy, done, joule, force, work, energy, more / greater, simple machines, levers, gears (either order)

B $120 \times 0.40 = 48\,\text{J}$

C **a** work done = force × distance = $1500 \times 1.0 = 1500\,\text{J}$

 b work done = $30 \times 50 = 1500\,\text{J}$

 c Ethan's chemical store empties, and the gravitational store of the load fills, as does the thermal store of Ethan's body and the surroundings; the amount lost from the chemical store is equal to the total gain in the gravitational and thermal stores

3.4.1

A temperature, thermometer, degrees Celsius, °C, same, equilibrium, no, more, thermal, mass, type (either order)

B **a** °C, stays the same, increases, move / vibrate, J, thermal, increases **b** less than

C   water, much larger mass

D   a   no – the person is warmer than their surroundings

   b   yes – tea has cooled to same temperature as room

   c   yes – thermometer has warmed to same temperature as mouth

3.4.2

A   thermal, hot, cooler / colder / cold, vibrate, conduction, solid, gaseous / gas, insulators, dense, dense, sinks, convection, convection current

B   4, 1, 2, 3

C   gases, thermal, far apart, weak, solids, non-metals, air

D   a vacuum has no particles to transfer energy from the room to the liquid by conduction or convection; so this cup takes the longest time to heat up and is the best insulator

3.4.3

A   conduction, convection (either order), radiation, infrared radiation, thermal imaging camera, absorb, transmitted / absorbed / reflected (any order) × 3, black / dark, matt / dull, white / light, shiny / glossy (either order)

B   a   conduction – particles vibrating; convection – particles moving; radiation – emission and absorption of infrared

   b   hot objects emit infrared radiation; when an object absorbs this radiation, it causes heating

   c   radiation reaches the Earth from the Sun through space, where there are no particles / which is a vacuum

C   large surface area allows more convection of nearby heated air to dissipate the thermal energy, also increases radiation; dull surface is good emitter, increases radiation

Big Idea 3 Pinchpoint

A   this is the correct answer

B   this is an incorrect answer – it describes **conduction** instead of convection, which is not the main process here

C   this is an incorrect answer – thermal energy or 'heat' is **not a substance**: it is important to focus on what is happening to the particles of the soup

D   this is an incorrect answer – the particles themselves do **not** expand, they just move further apart

Pinchpoint follow-up

A   the fan brings more cooler air into contact with the hot surface of the object; thermal energy is transferred from the object's store to the thermal energy store of the air and so is dissipated into the surroundings faster

B   conduction – when solid is heated, particles vibrate more, transmitting vibrations to their neighbours; convection – when liquid or gas is heated, particles move apart so that it becomes less dense and rises with the particles moving to a new position, transferring energy as they move; can only happen in liquids and gases; radiation – emission and absorption of infrared, can happen through a vacuum

C   4, 1, 2, 3, 5, 6

D   a   solid, liquid, liquid, gas, particles, arranged

   b   cold liquid – circles touching each other, packed close together so each circle touches several others; hot liquid – same sized circles still touching but spaced more, so that each circle touches only one or two others

4.3.1

A   compressions, rarefactions, pressure, microphone, loudspeaker, 20 000, ultrasound

B   a   the sound wave causes the whole diaphragm to vibrate in and out; this vibration causes the coil to move near the magnet; which varies the potential difference

   b   a loudspeaker inputs a changing potential difference (an electrical signal), and creates changes in air pressure; a microphone inputs changes in air pressure and creates a changing potential difference

C   higher, lower

D   Breanais: high waves generate more power

4.3.2

A   electromagnetic spectrum, visible light, Sun, wavelengths, high, high, wavelength, low, low, long, gamma, ionise, cancer, microwaves

B   e.g. radio waves – TV signals; microwaves – mobile phones, microwave ovens; infrared – heating, cooking; ultraviolet – detecting forgeries; X-rays – seeing broken bones; gamma rays – killing cancer cells

C   a   gamma rays, X-rays, ultraviolet, visible light, infrared, microwaves, radio waves

   b   arrow pointing to left, high frequency on left

D   a   the amount of energy transferred by electromagnetic radiation depends on frequency; only high-frequency parts of the spectrum, such as X-rays, transfer enough energy to cause ionisation, i.e. to remove electrons from atoms

   b   4, 1, 2, 3

4.4.1

A   wave, energy, transverse, longitudinal, transmission, superpose

B   a   fix one end of spring, bounce wave off it

   b   one bit of the spring oscillating causes the next bit to start oscillating

   c   pulse gets a bit smaller as it goes along because of friction

C   a   similarity: **one** from: vibration / oscillation, energy moves / travels in direction of wave, has wavelength / amplitude / frequency; difference: transverse – vibration at right angle to direction of wave travel / energy transfer, longitudinal – vibration parallel to direction of wave travel / energy transfer

   b   transverse – light / any electromagnetic wave, earthquake waves that cannot pass through liquid rock; longitudinal – sound / ultrasound, water wave, earthquake waves that can pass through liquid rock

D   a   if a peak and a trough arrive at same time, cancel out, add up to zero amplitude

   b   because **B** and light are both transverse waves

Big Idea 4 Pinchpoint

A   this is an incorrect answer – particles do **not** travel the whole length of a wave

B   this is an incorrect answer – in **longitudinal** waves the oscillations are parallel

C   this is an incorrect answer – waves **do** transfer energy, and energy **was** required to destroy the buildings

D   this is the correct answer

Pinchpoint follow-up

A   a   from left: oscillations, wavelength, energy transfer

   b   the particles oscillate across at right angles to the length of the spring, while energy is transferred along the spring

B   a   particles oscillate parallel to direction of wave

   b   particles oscillate at right angles to the direction of the wave

C   a   force, distance (moved), 1, transferred, force, distance, work, energy

   b   water waves, turbine, infrared, gamma ray, ionise

D   ground moves side to side or up and down, breaking the structure

Section 1 Revision questions

1 $200 \times 3000 = 600\,000$ [1] J [1]

2 a temperature [1], volume [1]   **b** pressure $= \dfrac{\text{force}}{\text{area}}$ [1]

    c i $1.8 \times 0.5 = 0.90\,\text{m}^2$ [1]

      ii $\dfrac{800}{0.90}$ [1] $= 890\,\text{N/m}^2$ [1] (to 2 sig. fig.)

      iii no, he will not sink as $890 < 20\,000\,\text{N/m}^2$ [1]

3 a transverse – oscillation (or motion of source or displacement) is at 90° (or right angles or perpendicular or normal) to the direction of the wave [1]; longitudinal – oscillation is parallel to direction of wave (or equivalent terms as above) [1]

    b

axes drawn and labelled [1], data plotted [1], best-fit curved line drawn [1]

4 radiation [1], shiny surfaces emit less infrared [1]

5 a C [1]

    b **six** from: diagram shows coil [1], diaphragm (cone) attached to coil [1], (permanent) magnet [1]; phone causes current in coil [1]; coil acts as electromagnet [1]; magnet causes magnetic force, pushing coil [1]; moves diaphragm (cone) in and out [1], emitting sound as it pushes air [1]

6 cup pushes particles of table closer together [1]; bonds between particles are compressed [1]; bonds between particles push back and support cup [1]

7 a i hot: Y, cold: X [1]   **ii** Y [1]

    b i hot air inside the balloon is less dense than the air around / outside the balloon [1], so the air inside the balloon has a smaller mass and weight than the air around / outside the balloon [1]

      ii long upwards arrow from middle of balloon, short downwards arrow from same place [1]

8 a $\dfrac{30}{1000} = 0.030\,\text{m}$ [1]; $8.0 \times 0.030 = 0.24\,\text{N m}$ [1]

    b moment is force times distance [1]; hand provides moment at handle [1]; equal moment applies to blades [1]; moving object closer means smaller distance, so force gets larger and cuts more easily [1]

9 car's weight pushes bridge's particles together [1]; bonds between bridge's particles are compressed [1]; bridge's particles push back and support the car [1]

10 a $\dfrac{1.2}{1500} = 0.000\,80$ [1] mm [1]; **or** $0.000\,000\,80$ [1] m [1]

    b all 9 points plotted correctly [2; 1 if only 7 points plotted correctly]; correct best-fit line for plotted points [1]

    c directly proportional **or** as force increases so does extension [1]

11 a increase [1] – larger current produces stronger magnetic field [1]

    b decrease [1] – each turn provides some magnetic field [1]

12 a conductor [1] – electrons free to move throughout metal [1]

    b insulator [1] – insulating material contains many trapped bubbles of air / gas [1]

13 a incorrect [1] – liquids are not compressible [1]

    b incorrect [1] – surface at lower pressure than deep ocean [1]

    c correct [1] – surface at lower pressure than deep ocean [1]

14 six from: when absorbed, an X-ray transfers enough energy [1] to remove an electron from an atom [1]; this can damage molecules such as DNA [1], possibly causing cancer [1]; the energy absorbed from radiation depends on its frequency (or wavelength) [1]; microwaves have a lower frequency (higher wavelength) than X-rays (or converse) [1] so their energy is too low to cause ionisation [1]

15 a energy is always transferred from a hot object (air) to a cold object (ice cream) [1]; the temperature of ice cream will become the same as the temperature of the air [1]

    b air **particles** are **vibrating / moving** faster than ice cream **particles** [1]; air particles **collide** with / touch ice cream particles [1]; energy is **transferred** from the **thermal energy** store of air to the thermal energy store of ice cream [1], raising the **temperature** of ice cream and lowering the temperature of the air [1]

    c silvered / shiny paper is a good reflector of thermal energy from air [1]; air is trapped between wrapping and cone – air is a good insulator [1]

5.3.1

A substances, elements, Periodic, chemical, symbol

B a 1, 4, 5, 8

    b 2 – It is **not** possible to break down an element into other substances. 3 – There are **98** / about **100** naturally occurring elements. 6 – The chemical symbol of sodium is **Na**. 7 – The chemical symbol of bromine is **Br**.

C hydrogen; C; nitrogen; O; sodium, Mg; aluminium; S; chlorine; K; iron; Cu; zinc; Br; iodine; W

D to avoid confusion / to enable chemists to communicate about elements, whatever language they normally use

5.3.2

A atoms, smallest, atoms, different, many

B a 2, 5

    b 1 – an atom is the smallest part of an element that can exist; 3 – the atoms of copper are different from the atoms of zinc; 4 – a single atom of zinc does not have the same properties as a piece of zinc wire

C a as copper melts, its atoms move out of their fixed positions; they no longer vibrate on the spot, but instead move around from place to place, sliding over each other

    b one copper atom on its own cannot melt because the properties of copper as a solid and liquid are the properties of many atoms; melting involves a change

D a $12 \div 6 = 2$
600 000 million million million $\div 2 = 300\,000$ million million million

    b $24 \div 12 = 2$
600 000 million million million $\times 2 = 1\,200\,000$ million million million

    c $\dfrac{60\,000 \text{ million million million}}{600\,000 \text{ million million million}} = 0.1$
$0.1 \times 12\,\text{g} = 1.2\,\text{g}$

5.3.3

A elements, strongly, different, one, atoms, strongly, atom, atoms

B **a** **T**, **V**, **W**, **X**, **Z**

    b they include atoms of more than one element; the atoms of the different elements are joined together

C **a** 2   **b** 3   **c** 1   **d** 2

D **a** all 3 are solid at room temperature

    b **two** from: their melting points are different, the appearance of sulfur is different from the appearance of iron sulfide, iron is attracted to a magnet but iron sulfide is not

    c in iron sulfide the atoms are joined together to make one new substance

5.3.4

A chemical, number, oxygen, one

B from top: MgO; one atom of calcium for every two atoms of chlorine; nitrogen dioxide; one atom of carbon for every one atom of oxygen, CO; one atom of sulfur for every three atoms of oxygen; sulfur trioxide, one atom of sulfur for every three atoms of oxygen

C 2, 3, 4, 5, 3, 3

D **a** $2 \times 16 = 32$ **b** $(2 \times 1) + 16 = 18$

    c $(13 \times 12) + (18 \times 1) + (2 \times 16) = 206$

    d relative mass of carbon atoms shown in formula = $13 \times 12 = 156$; relative mass of hydrogen atoms shown in formula = $18 \times 1 = 18$; relative mass of oxygen atoms shown in formula = $2 \times 16 = 32$. Answer is carbon

5.3.5

A long, many, many, different, atoms

B **a** it is strong, very flexible, and waterproof

    b nylon is stronger than poly(propene)

    c HDPE and rigid PVC; reasons both are rigid and waterproof

    d both are flexible and waterproof; flexible PVC has a greater strength than LDPE when pulled, by 5 MPa; the density of flexible PVC is $(1.30 - 0.92) = 0.38$ g/cm³ greater than the density of LDPE

C polymer **X** is flexible because the molecules can slide over each other; polymer **Y** is rigid because the links that join the long molecules together stop the long molecules sliding over each other

D advantages of wood – renewable, biodegradable, attractive; disadvantage of wood – can be damaged by water (can rot); advantages of HDPE – easy to clean, waterproof; does not rot; disadvantages of HDPE – made from a non-renewable resource (oil); difficult to dispose of since it is non-biodegradable

5.4.1

A groups, periods, groups, periods, group / period

B **a** density = $\dfrac{\text{mass}}{\text{volume}} = \dfrac{56.6\,\text{g}}{5.0\,\text{cm}^3} = 11.3$ g/cm³

    b density increases from top to bottom of both groups; the patterns for both groups are similar

C **a** in Period 4, melting point increases from left to right for elements in first two groups, and then decreases; in Period 5, melting point increases from left to right for elements in first three groups, and then decreases

    b melting point – greater than 1850 °C and less than 3000 °C (actual value is 2220 °C); reason – if patterns in Periods 5 and 6 are the same, Hf has a lower melting point than Ta; if patterns in all groups shown are the same, Hf has a greater melting point than Zr

5.4.2

A left, conduct, low, reactive, two / new, hydrogen, hydroxide

B **a** boiling point decreases gradually from lithium (about 1330 °C) at the top of the group to rubidium (about 690 °C) at the bottom of the group

    b for each element, boiling point is greater than melting point; both melting point and boiling point decrease from top to bottom of the group

    c any value below 39 °C (actual value is 29 °C)

C **a** element burns in chlorine; product is a white solid

    b white solid

    c caesium chloride

5.4.3

A right, halogens, metals, reactions

B top symbol – corrosive, burns eyes, wear eye protection; lower symbol – toxic, difficulty breathing, use fume cupboard

C top row: **V**, **X**; middle row: **Y**, **W**; bottom row: **Y**, **Y**

D **a** above bromine

    b only a halogen that is above bromine in Group 7, and is therefore more reactive, can displace bromine from its compounds

5.4.4

A right, noble, metals, unreactive (inert)

B **a** 3   **b** 3   **c** 1   **d** 2

    b all group 0 elements unreactive; reactivity increases from top to bottom of group

C **a** increases from top to bottom

    b any value between −189 °C and −112 °C (actual value is −157 °C); trend shows that melting point increases from top to bottom, so value for krypton is likely to be between the values of the elements immediately above and below it in the group

D group 1 – boiling points decrease from top to bottom of group and all boiling points are above 0 °C; group 0 – boiling points increase from top to bottom of group and all boiling points are below 0 °C

Big Idea 5 Pinchpoint

A this is an incorrect answer – the Group 7 element on its own (bromine) is **less reactive** than the one in the compound (fluorine) so no displacement reaction occurs

B this is the correct answer

C this is an incorrect answer – a reaction only occurs if the element on its own (bromine) is **more** reactive than the element in the compound (chlorine); bromine is **less** reactive than chlorine, so no reaction occurs

D this is an incorrect answer – chlorine is below fluorine in Group 7, so chlorine is **less** reactive than fluorine; a displacement reaction can only occur if the element on its own is **more** reactive than the element in the compound

Pinchpoint follow-up

A **a** bromine, chlorine, fluorine, chlorine

    b **i** bromine + potassium iodide; fluorine + potassium chloride; chlorine + potassium iodide

       ii bromine + potassium iodide → potassium bromide + iodine; fluorine + potassium chloride → potassium fluoride + chlorine; chlorine + potassium iodide → potassium chloride + iodine

B **a** fluorine and potassium chloride; chlorine and potassium iodide; fluorine and potassium bromide

    b fluorine + potassium chloride → potassium fluoride + chlorine; chlorine + potassium iodide → potassium chloride + iodine; fluorine + potassium bromide → potassium fluoride + bromine

C A displacement reaction occurs between a pair of substances if the **more** reactive Group 7 element is on its own, and if the **less** reactive Group 7 element is part of a compound. Fluorine is more reactive than chlorine. This means that fluorine and potassium **do** react together in a displacement reaction. Iodine is **less** reactive than bromine. This means that potassium iodide and bromine react together in a **displacement** reaction. The products are iodine and potassium **bromide**.

D **a** fluorine, chlorine, bromine, iodine
   b 1, 4, 6, 8
   c 2 – Fluorine **reacts** with potassium chloride. 3 – Iodine is **less** reactive than bromine. 5 – Chlorine is **more** reactive than iodine. 7 – Fluorine is the **most** reactive element in group 7.

6.3.1

A reactants, products, left, right, atoms, differently, after
B **a** sulfur + oxygen → sulfur dioxide
   b sodium + chlorine → sodium chloride
   c methane + oxygen → carbon dioxide + water
C **a** methane and oxygen
   b carbon dioxide and water
   c 1, 1; 4, 4; 4, 4
   d the atoms are rearranged and join together differently
D three of the carbon atoms have joined to two oxygen atoms each to make carbon dioxide – these atoms have been rearranged and joined together differently; the arrangement of nine of the carbon atoms has not changed, showing that some of the carbon has remained unchanged / unreacted

6.3.2

A energy, combustion, oxygen, carbon dioxide, water, oxygen
B **a** from top row: carbon dioxide, carbon dioxide; water, oxygen; carbon dioxide and water, oxygen, carbon dioxide
   b product of combustion of hydrogen is harmless water; products of combustion of heptane are harmless water and carbon dioxide, which is a greenhouse gas that contributes to global warming
C **a** volume of water – control; increase in temperature of water – dependent; fuel – independent; distance of flame from test tube – control
   b place a shield around the apparatus to reduce the amount of energy transferred to the surroundings instead of to the water

6.3.3

A one, two, compound, compounds, oxide, carbon dioxide, thermal
B **a** Y
   b one reactant breaks down to make two products
C **a** lead carbonate → lead oxide + carbon dioxide
   b they decompose to make the metal oxide and carbon dioxide
   c strontium oxide, nitrogen dioxide, and oxygen
D potassium carbonate did not decompose under the conditions of the investigation; copper carbonate decomposed most easily; lead carbonate did decompose, but less easily than copper carbonate

6.3.4

A physical, same, products, conservation, reactants
B **a** the same numbers of each type of atom are present before and after the reaction
   b $2H_2 + O_2 \rightarrow 2H_2O$
C **a** 44 g   **b** 4.4 g   **c** 11.2 g

D **a** mass does not change   **b** mass increases
   c mass decreases   **d** mass does not change
   e in **b**, the mass of solid at the start is the mass of magnesium; magnesium joins with oxygen gas from the air (which has mass) to make a solid product, magnesium oxide; this means that the mass of solid product is greater than the mass of solid reactant in **d**, both reactants are in the solid state, and so are both products; this means that the total mass of solid reactants is equal to the total mass of solid products

6.4.1

A energy, from, to, increase, from, to, decrease, energy, exothermic, endothermic
B **a** from top: 58, 8
   b the temperatures of both reacting mixtures increase at first, showing that the reactions are exothermic; the temperature change for magnesium is 8 °C, which is greater than the temperature change for zinc (5 °C) so the reaction with magnesium is more exothermic
C **a** aluminium chloride and magnesium chloride
   b aluminium chloride, magnesium chloride; on dissolving, they transfer energy to the surroundings / hands, so warming them up

6.4.2

A products, after, exothermic, endothermic
B 2, 3
C e.g. all three substances transfer energy to the surroundings when they burn; per gram, hydrogen transfers approximately three times as much energy to the surroundings as petrol; ethanol transfers the least energy to the surroundings
D **a** top: solute / substance **X** and solvent; bottom: solution (of substance **X**)
   b energy transferred to the surroundings
   c heating food, since energy is transferred to the surroundings / food

6.4.3

A break, endothermic, products, exothermic, more, less, catalyst
B **a** **X** – energy needed to break bonds; **Y** – energy given out when new bonds are made; **Z** – overall energy change for the reaction
   b the energy required to break bonds in the reactants is more than the energy released when new bonds are made in the products; overall the chemical reaction transfers energy **from** the surroundings, so it is endothermic
C **a** 436 + 243 = 679 kJ/mol
   b 2 × 432 = 864 kJ/mol
   c exothermic, since the energy released on making new bonds in the product is greater than the energy required to break the bonds in the reactants

Big Idea 6 Pinchpoint

A this is an incorrect answer – a mass has gas, so when a gas leaves a reacting mixture, the mass of the reacting mixture **decreases**
B this is an incorrect answer – if one of the products of a reactant is in the gas state, the mass of solid reactants is **less** than the mass of solid products
C this is an incorrect answer – in chemical reactions, atoms are rearranged and join together differently; the **total mass does not increase** when new substances are made
D this is the correct answer

Pinchpoint follow-up

A 1, 4
B from top: decreases, decreases, increases, decreases, increases, does not change

C **a** The mass of a nitrogen atom in the product is **the same as** the mass of a nitrogen atom in the reactants.

b The mass of an oxygen atom in the product is **the same as** the mass of an oxygen atom in the reactants.

c In the chemical reaction, the atoms **are** rearranged.

d In the chemical reaction, the atoms are joined together **differently** before and after the reaction.

e There are the **same number** of atoms in the reactants as in the products.

f The total mass of products is **the same as** the total mass of reactants.

D **a** solid magnesium reacts with oxygen gas from the air, so the mass of solid product is equal to the mass of solid magnesium plus the mass of oxygen that reacts with it

b a gas is produced, so the mass of solid product is equal to the mass of solid lead carbonate minus the mass of carbon dioxide that was produced and escaped to the air

c all the reactants and products are in the solid state; none of the reactants or products is in the gas state, so the total mass of substance in the reaction vessel does not change

d on warming hydrogen peroxide, oxygen gas is produced, so the mass of product that remains in the reaction vessel is equal to the mass of solution at the start minus the mass of oxygen that was produced and escaped to the air

7.3.1

A atmosphere, transferred, dioxide, temperature

B from left: 3, 2, 4, 1

C **a** the transfer of energy from the Sun to the thermal store of gases in the atmosphere

b the gradual increase in the surface temperature of the Earth

D 2

7.3.2

A sinks / reservoirs, sedimentary, fossil, cycle, respire, burn / combust, photosynthesis, dissolving, same, change / increase / decrease

B

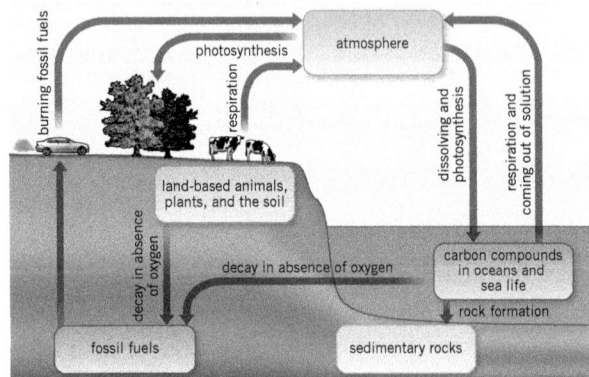

C **a** carbon dioxide was added to the atmosphere (by respiration and combustion) at the same rate as it left it (by photosynthesis and dissolving in the oceans)

b carbon dioxide was added to the atmosphere faster (by respiration and increasing combustion) than it left it (by photosynthesis and dissolving in the oceans)

c from the atmosphere, by photosynthesis

7.3.3

A cycle, carbon, temperature, warming, warming, ice, weather, climate, species, food

B deforestation – less carbon dioxide is removed from the atmosphere; burning fossil fuels – more carbon dioxide goes into the atmosphere; every year, more carbon dioxide is added to the atmosphere than is removed – the concentration of carbon dioxide in the atmosphere increases; climate change – glaciers melt, some plant and animal species become extinct, it is harder for humans in some areas to grow enough food

C column 1 – 1, 2, 7; column 2 – 4, 5; column 3 – 3, 6, 8

D e.g. **benefits** – less carbon dioxide and methane will enter the atmosphere, smaller area of land will be cleared of forests to provide grazing land for cattle; fewer animals will be killed for meat; **disadvantages** – many people like eating meat; people might not eat enough protein; humans cannot digest grass, so food cannot be obtained from land that is unsuitable for growing crops (unless sheep or goats are grazed on the land instead); an **overall decision** is also required in the answer

7.4.1

A crust, mixed, ore, below, electrolysis

B zinc – ✓ – zinc is lower in reactivity series than carbon, so can be displaced from its compounds by carbon; magnesium – ✗ – magnesium is higher in reactivity series than carbon, so cannot be displaced from its compounds by carbon; lead – ✓ – lead is lower in reactivity series than carbon, so can be displaced from its compounds by carbon

C **a** e.g. price that the aluminium can be sold for; cost of extracting aluminium

b e.g. using the waste produce for a useful purpose

c e.g. generating the electricity using solar power, wind turbines, geothermal energy, or water / hydroelectricity

7.4.2

A processing, reducing

B 1, 6, 5, 4, 2, 3

C advantages – producing aluminium from recycling requires less energy than producing it from aluminium ore; recycling results in less waste solid than producing it from ore; supplies of aluminium ore will last longer; disadvantages – some people do not like sorting their waste, and the lorries that collect cans for recycling produce polluting / greenhouse gases; overall judgement given, with reasons

D **a** e.g. less plastic waste produced; smaller amount of fossil fuels / raw materials used

b e.g. making items from other materials instead of plastic; making plastic items more expensive

Big Idea 7 Pinchpoint

A this is the correct answer

B this is an incorrect answer – rubidium and beryllium are above carbon in the reactivity series, which shows that they are **more** reactive than carbon

C this is an incorrect answer – only metals that are **less** reactive than carbon can be extracted from their compounds by heating with carbon

D this is an incorrect answer – only metals that are **less** reactive than carbon can be extracted from their compounds by heating with carbon

Pinchpoint follow-up

A **a** sodium; $TiCl_4 + 4Na \rightarrow Ti + 4NaCl$

b aluminium; $Cr_2O_3 + 2Al \rightarrow Al_2O_3 + 2Cr$

c hydrogen; $WO_3 + 3H_2 \rightarrow W + 3H_2O$

B **a** most reactive – rubidium; least reactive – nickel

b most reactive – potassium; least reactive – chromium

c most reactive – barium; least reactive – copper

d most reactive – rubidium; least reactive – strontium

e most reactive – chromium; least reactive – copper

C **a** 4   **b** 5   **c** 3   **d** 6

D The reactivity series lists metals in order of reactivity. Metals at the **top** are more reactive than metals at the **bottom**. Carbon is also included in the reactivity series, even though it is not a metal; If a metal is **below** carbon in the reactivity series, it is less reactive than carbon. A metal that is **less** reactive than carbon may be extracted from its compounds by heating with carbon. A **displacement** reaction occurs. The word equations below show examples of displacement reactions in which a metal is extracted from a compound by heating with **carbon**: tin oxide + carbon → tin oxide + carbon dioxide lead oxide + carbon dioxide → lead + carbon dioxide6

Section 2 Revision questions

1 from top: C [1], Cl [1], sodium [1], Fe [1], tungsten [1]
2 from top – a pure element; a mixture of two compounds; a mixture of an element and a compound; a mixture of two elements [3 if all correct; 2 if 2 or 3 correct; 1 if 1 correct]
3 **a** a substance made up of atoms of two or more elements, strongly joined together [1]
  b gallium and arsenic [1]
  c gallium + arsenic → gallium arsenide [1]
4 **a** 4 [1] **b** 8 + 10 + 4 + 2 [1] = 24 [1]
5 **a** the substance is a compound made up of atoms of two elements [1]; there are two atoms of silver for every one atom of sulfur in the compound [1]
  b silver sulfide consists of particles of two elements, strongly joined together in a compound, but silver and sulfur each have particles of one element only [1]
6 **a** exothermic, since energy is transferred to the surroundings [1]
  b decrease [1] because the product is formed as a gas, and escapes to the surroundings [1]
7 for many years: respiration and burning of fossil fuels added carbon dioxide to atmosphere [1]; photosynthesis and dissolving in oceans removed carbon dioxide from the atmosphere [1]; rates at which carbon dioxide was added to and removed from the atmosphere were the same [1]; since 1960: more fossil fuels burnt by humans, resulting in more carbon dioxide being added to atmosphere [1]; deforestation, resulting in less carbon dioxide being removed from atmosphere [1]; rate at which carbon dioxide added to atmosphere now greater than rate at which it is removed [1]
8 e.g. rising mean global temperatures leads to melting ice [1] and flooding of low-lying land [1]; **or** rising mean global temperatures leads to climate change, including more frequent droughts in some areas [1] which may lead to crop failures [1]
9 **a** $\frac{45\,kg}{500\,kg} \times 100$ [1] = 9% [1]
  b **i** carbon dioxide [1]
    ii carbon dioxide is a greenhouse gas [1]
10 **a** density increases from top to bottom [1]
  b any answer between 5.91 and 11.8 g/cm³ (actual density is 7.30) [1]
  c predicted density is between values for gallium and thallium [1]
11 **a** one reactant breaks down into two or more simpler compounds or elements [1]
  b the gas is both corrosive and toxic [1]; the teacher could not take safety precautions to adequately protect students from the dangers associated with these hazards [1]
  c **i** the substances are in the gas state, so their particles are moving around from place to place within the whole container [1]; since the test tube is open, some gas particles escape from it [1]
    ii 2.76 g – 0.60 g [1] = 2.16 g [1]
  d 2, 4 [1; both needed for mark]
12 $\frac{0.4\,g}{4\,g} \times 600\,000$ million million million [1]
  = 60 000 million million million [1]
13 $4Li(s) + O_2(g) \rightarrow 2Li_2O(s)$ [1 for correct balancing, 1 for correct state symbols]

14 in Group 1, melting point decreases from top to bottom [1] but in Group 0, it increases from top to bottom [1]; all the Group 1 elements conduct electricity [1] but none of the Group 0 elements do [1]; the Group 1 elements are very reactive [1] but the Group 0 elements are unreactive / inert [1]

8.3.1

A respiratory, lungs, oxygen, exhale, trachea, bronchi / bronchus, alveoli / alveolus, gas exchange
B 1 trachea; 2 lungs; 3 rib; 4 diaphragm; 5 bronchus; 6 bronchiole; 7 alveoli
C they maximise diffusion of gases between the lungs and the blood by having: a large number – to create a large surface area; thin walls – only one cell thick; a rich blood supply – to transport gases to / away from the lungs
D **a** higher percentage in exhaled air as it is a waste product of respiration
  b lower percentage in exhaled air as some is used in respiration
  c percentages are the same, as the gas is not used or produced by the body

8.3.2

A ribs, contract, increases, decreases, relax, decreases, increases, out, bell jar, asthma, volume
B muscles between ribs contract, pulling the ribcage up and out; the diaphragm contracts and moves down; the volume inside the chest increases; so the pressure decreases; this draws air into the lungs through the trachea
C **a** push the rubber sheet up to represent the diaphragm relaxing; the volume inside the chest decreases so the air pressure increases; air is forced out of the balloons (which represent the lungs) so they deflate
  b the ribcage / bell jar wall doesn't move, which would further decrease the volume of chest cavity
D (fill a plastic bottle with water and place a plastic tube in the neck of the bottle; turn the bottle of water upside down in a tank of water); read the level of water in the bottle; take a deep breath, then breathe out for as long as possible into the tube; read the new level of water in the bottle; calculate the difference in the water levels – this is your lung volume

8.3.3

A drugs, recreational, medicinal, addiction, withdrawal symptoms
B **a** taken to benefit health / cure diseases / treat symptoms – e.g. antibiotic / paracetamol / aspirin
  b taken for enjoyment / have no health benefit – e.g. ecstasy / caffeine / alcohol / tobacco
C **a** liver / brain **b** lung / mouth **c** speeds up
D **a** to kill bacteria / treat bacterial infection
  b to relieve pain
E withdrawal symptoms make stopping harder / socially withdrawn / increased crime for money / infection spread through needles

8.3.4

A ethanol, nervous, depressant, liver, unit, alcoholic(s)
B **a** liver, brain
  b between 1991 and 2008, the number of alcohol-related deaths has increased from 9 per 100 000 of the population to 19 per 100 000 of the population
C **a** alcohol reduces sperm production, so decreases likelihood of conception
  b diffuses into baby's blood damaging organs and nervous system causing foetal alcohol syndrome (FAS) / learning difficulties / still or premature birth

8.3.5

A cancer / disease, heart, passive, airways, monoxide, oxygen, stimulant, miscarriage

B **a** sticky black material that collects in lungs and contains chemicals that can cause cancer

b gas that binds to red blood cells, stopping them from carrying as much oxygen

c stimulant that speeds up the nervous system / makes heart beat faster / narrows blood vessels

C the more cigarettes smoked, the greater the risk of lung cancer (does not mean you will get disease); approximately linear correlation

D chemicals in tobacco smoke stop cilia moving, so mucus containing dirt and microorganisms flows more freely into the lungs where microorganisms can cause an infection

E increases risk of miscarriage / low birth weight and affects foetal development

8.4.1

A balanced, nutrients, carbohydrates, lipids (either order), proteins, vitamins, minerals (either order), fibre

B carbohydrate – main source of energy; lipid – store of energy / keep you warm / protect organs: protein – growth and repair of body tissues; vitamins and minerals – keep you healthy

C adds bulk to your food, which keeps it moving through intestines; waste is pushed out of the body more easily / prevents constipation

D baked beans – more fibre / less salt / less fat (less carbohydrate – depending on the person's energy requirements)

8.4.2

A food tests, iodine, starch, red, purple, protein, cloudy

B starch – iodine; lipid – ethanol; simple sugar – Benedict's solution; protein – copper sulfate and sodium hydroxide (Biuret solution)

C rub on filter / greaseproof / brown paper, hold up to the light, goes translucent

D **a** **X** and **Y** **b** **Y** and **Z** **c** sugar and lipids

d sample **Y** – animal products do not contain starch / milk contains lipids, sugar (lactose), and protein

e e.g. possible allergies / presence of lipids / sugar may not be wanted if on a calorie-controlled diet

8.4.3

A malnourishment, underweight, deficiency, starvation, fat, obese

B tiredness / poor immune system / lack of energy / (named) vitamin deficiency

C diabetes / heart disease / stroke / some cancers

D **a** **i** $15\,000 - 10\,000 = 5000\,kJ$

ii more labour-intensive profession so more energy is required for movement / use of muscles

b **i** $11\,000 - 9000 = 2000; \dfrac{2000}{11\,000} \times 100 = 22.2\%$

ii extra energy required to support growing baby

E if you take in more energy that you use (through eating too much food, or too much fatty food) you gain body mass; this is stored as fat under the skin and can result in obesity

8.4.4

A digestive system, gullet, stomach, acids, digestion, small, large, rectum, anus

B clockwise from top: gullet, stomach, large intestine, rectum, small intestine

C stomach – where food is mixed with digestive juices and acids; large intestine – water reabsorbed, only solid undigested food / faeces remain

D thin wall – to speed up diffusion / absorption; covered in villi – increase surface area; rich blood supply – carry away absorbed food molecules (maintain diffusion gradient)

E large food molecules are broken into small molecules; these can be absorbed through the wall of the small intestine and transported in blood to where needed in the body

8.4.5

A bacteria, vitamins, enzymes, catalyst, carbohydrase, sugar, protease, protein, lipase, glycerol, bile

B **a** **X** and **Y** **b** Enzymes are made of proteins. Enzymes are not used up during a reaction

C *carbohydrase* – carbohydrate – sugars; lipase – *lipid* – fatty acids and glycerol; protease – protein – *amino acids*

D **a** large intestine **b** fibre

c make vitamins such as vitamin K which are absorbed by the body to keep you healthy

Big Idea 8 Pinchpoint

A this is an incorrect answer – **muscles** in the wall of the intestine move the food along the gut

B this is an incorrect answer – digestion **and** absorption are carried out in the small intestine

C this is the correct answer

D this is an incorrect answer – the wall of the small intestine is **not** smooth, it is covered in villi

Pinchpoint follow-up

A fibre, bulk, muscles, wall, push against, squeezing a tube of toothpaste, soluble, small, speeds up, faeces, rectum

B **a** carbohydrates into sugar molecules, proteins into amino acids, lipids into fatty acids and glycerol

b mouth – carbohydrase, stomach – carbohydrase, protease, small intestine – carbohydrase, protease, lipase

C **a** carbohydrates

b reduced surface area for absorption; reduction in absorption of digested food particles; person malnourished / suffers from a deficiency causing e.g. tiredness, named deficiency condition (calcium / iron / B_{12})

D **a** **i** 3 **ii** 1 **iii** 2

b maintains a concentration gradient / ensures that the blood always has a lower concentration of a food molecule than the intestine so digested food molecules diffuse down concentration gradient / from high to low concentration

9.3.1

A aerobic respiration, glucose, mitochondria, water, carbohydrates, plasma, diffuses, haemoglobin

B oxygen, carbon dioxide

C **a** mitochondria

b need to transfer lots of energy to contract (to effect movement)

D **a** **i** number of repeats of named exercise / activity

ii breathing rate / number of breaths in named time

iii length of activity

b as exercise level increases, breathing rate increases as more oxygen needs to be taken to cells for respiration, to transfer more energy for movement

E **a** food is broken down during digestion releasing glucose; glucose absorbed through wall of small intestine into blood stream where it dissolves into plasma; carried around the body and diffuses into cells that need it

b during inhalation, air enters the lungs and oxygen diffuses into blood stream through alveoli; oxygen joins to haemoglobin in red blood cells and is carried around the body; it then diffuses into the cells that need it

9.3.2

A anaerobic respiration, lactic acid, oxygen debt, fermentation, ethanol

B glucose → lactic acid

C **a** glucose → ethanol + carbon dioxide
   b microorganisms / named microorganism, e.g. yeast

D aerobic: glucose is a reactant; oxygen is a reactant; carbon dioxide is produced; water is produced; anaerobic: glucose is a reactant; lactic acid is produced

E **a** aerobic respiration transfers more energy per glucose molecule, anaerobic respiration can cause painful muscle cramps
   b when they require a lot of energy quickly, e.g. to escape from danger

9.3.3

A yeast, beer / other alcoholic drink, fermentation, ethanol, enzymes, faster / quicker

B glucose, ethanol

C 3, 4, 2, 5, 1

D the ethanol produced during fermentation evaporates when the dough is baked

E warm, good supply of glucose, and yeast

F enzymes in yeast speed up the rate of fermentation; therefore the higher the temperature, the faster the rate of fermentation (as there will be more collisions between enzymes and substrates); however, above a certain temperature, the enzymes will be damaged and no longer work

9.4.1

A algae, producers, photosynthesis, consumers, water, glucose, chlorophyll

B **a** water, light, oxygen   **b** glucose and oxygen
   c carbon dioxide and water

C **a** diffuses through tiny holes / stomata on underside of leaf
   b diffuses into root hair cells from soil
   c absorbed by chlorophyll in chloroplasts

D **a** water enters plant through roots, via root hair cells, which increase surface area to maximise uptake; water is transported to the leaves, via the stem; the stem contains long hollow tubes called xylem
   b water is lost from the leaves via evaporation, and is used in photosynthesis; evaporation occurs at night, even when the plant is not using water for photosynthesis

E the greater the rate of producer photosynthesis, the greater the biomass increase; more food available for primary consumer; more organisms available for next level of food chain

9.4.2

A leaves, stomata, carbon dioxide, oxygen, veins, palisade, chloroplasts

B clockwise from top-left – waxy layer, chloroplast, palisade layer, spongy layer, air space, guard cell, stoma

C **a** transport water and glucose to cells in leaf
   b reduces water loss through evaporation
   c open and close stomata
   d allow gases to diffuse into and out of leaf

D most chloroplasts found in the top of leaf in palisade layer as this is the area of the leaf which receives most sunlight; this therefore maximises amount of sunlight absorbed by chlorophyll in chloroplasts, maximising photosynthesis

E thin – allows carbon dioxide to diffuse in to maximise photosynthesis (and oxygen to diffuse out); large surface area maximises the amount of sunlight which can be absorbed to maximise photosynthesis

9.4.3

A iodine, blue-black, oxygen / gas, light, carbon dioxide, temperature, increases

B **a** 4, 5, 3, 1, 2
   b white areas of the leaf do not contain chlorophyll; therefore no photosynthesis occurs so starch isn't made

C

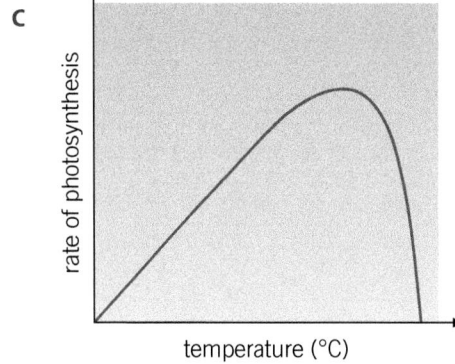

initially, increasing the temperature increases the rate of photosynthesis, because enzymes work faster in warmer conditions (as collision frequency between particles increases); at high temperatures, enzymes are damaged / stop working so photosynthesis stops

D by counting the number of oxygen bubbles given off / measuring the volume of oxygen produced in a set time; the more oxygen produced, the faster the plant is photosynthesising

9.4.4

A minerals, magnesium, potassium, nitrates, phosphates, deficiency, fertilisers

B nitrate – healthy growth – poor growth, older leaves are yellowed; phosphate – healthy roots – poor root growth, younger leaves look purple; potassium – healthy leaves and flowers – yellow leaves with dead patches; magnesium – making chlorophyll – plant leaves turn yellow

C **a** magnesium   **b** chlorophyll, which makes a plant green, contains magnesium, so if a plant has a magnesium deficiency it won't produce much / any chlorophyll, so leaves are not green

D **a** 31 cm   **b** no: results are too similar for B and C; the scientist would need to look for other symptoms such as purple leaves to distinguish which seedlings were grown in the dummy supplement

Big Idea 9 Pinchpoint

A this is an incorrect answer – this is the word equation for **aerobic respiration**

B this is an incorrect answer – plants **do not** breathe as they do not have lungs; gas exchange occurs in the leaf

C this is an incorrect answer – minerals are **not** needed for photosynthesis but do help a plant to remain healthy

D this is the correct answer

Pinchpoint follow-up

A **a** carbon dioxide and water underlined
   b glucose and oxygen circled
   c carbon dioxide + water $\xrightarrow{\text{light}}$ glucose + oxygen

B leaves, stomata, carbon dioxide, oxygen, photosynthesis, stomata, energy

C **a** dish 4
   b water is required for photosynthesis (so both seedlings 2 and 4 remained alive); seedling 4 also had access to minerals from the soil, which are needed for healthy growth

D **a** as light intensity increases, the rate of photosynthesis increases until it reaches a maximum at a relative light intensity of 6
   b light is required for photosynthesis
   c rate of photosynthesis is 9.0, as another factor is now limiting the rate of reaction (accept suggested variable e.g. availability of water)

10.3.1

A evolved, millions, natural selection, survive, genes, fossils
B 4, 6, 2, 5, 1, 3
C **a** remains or traces of animals that lived many years ago
   b evidence of species that are now extinct, e.g. dinosaurs
D named example, e.g. peppered moth; before industrial revolution, more pale moths, camouflaged against pale bark so survived and reproduced (dark moths seen and eaten); after revolution, dark moths increased as camouflaged against soot on bark; population evolved to be predominantly dark

10.3.2

A Darwin, evolve, selection, beaks, reproduce, peer, Wallace
B a scientist (working in the same area of study) reads and evaluates another scientist's work; if they agree with the findings, the work can then be published
C fossil record – organisms have changed over time (millions of years); extinction – species that do not adapt to environmental changes die out; development of antibiotic-resistant bacteria – microorganisms best suited for their environment survive and reproduce
D he found that birds living on different islands had different shaped / sized beaks and claws, and that these were linked to the different food available to eat; he concluded that a bird, born with a beak adapted for the food source available, would survive and reproduce producing more birds with this shape of beak; others would die / not survive to reproduce; over time, all the birds would have the beak most suited to the food source; this was his theory of natural selection

10.3.3

A biodiversity, habitats, disease, extinct, endangered
B **a** e.g. woodland / coral reef
   b e.g. desert / single-crop field
   c in an area of high biodiversity, if one species of plant is destroyed there will be many others available for food / shelter; this means other populations of organism will survive; however, in an area of low biodiversity, if one species of plant is destroyed, there may not be another for other populations to feed on; so other species are more likely to die
C **three** from: outbreak of a new disease – organisms killed by a microorganism; introduction of new competitors – lack of food; environmental change – drought; destruction of habitat / deforestation – loss of food / shelter

10.3.4

A endangered, conservation, captive, banks, survives
B conservation – protecting a natural environment – increases organisms' chance of survival; captive breeding – breeding animals in human-controlled environments – creates a healthy stable population; gene banks – store genetic samples – material can be used for research
C **a** **two** from: protects individuals so they are more likely to survive; live longer; mates provided so more likely to reproduce, increasing the population; animals can be reintroduced into wild
   b **two** from: animals may not survive if released, e.g. don't know how to hunt; loss of genetic biodiversity / problems of inbreeding; animals have less space / boredom

D conservation of the tigers' habitat – e.g. by preventing poaching / trees being removed; this increases tigers' chance of survival and reproduction which will result in more offspring and an increase in population number

10.4.1

A nucleus, DNA, chromosomes, genes
B egg and sperm drawn each containing 23 chromosomes, combining to make a fertilised egg with 46 chromosomes
C a gene holds the information to produce a specific characteristic (or protein) such as eye colour
D **a** change in the DNA
   b mutation has to occur in a gamete / sperm / egg cell

10.4.2

A nucleus, two, helix, bases, Franklin, X-rays, Watson, helical / helix
B **three** from: DNA is made up of two strand; the strands are twisted together to form a double helix; the strands are joined together by chemical bases; the bases are adenine (A), thymine (T), guanine (G), and cytosine (C)
C characteristics, pea, nucleus, DNA, structure, helix, working, sharing, discoveries
D **two** from: confirm the outcomes from an investigation; gather additional data; combine different areas of research; make use of different technology; other appropriate suggestion that would provide more evidence to confirm or disprove a hypothesis

10.4.3

A alleles, dominant, recessive, Punnett
B freckles, freckles, no freckles
C **a** all cells in Punnett square: Bb; all / 100% black fur
   b

	Female	
	B	b
B	BB	Bb
B	Bb	bb

Male (left label)

75% black fur, 25% white fur

D

	Mother	
	D	d
D	DD	Dd
d	Dd	dd

Father (left label)

both parents have one dominant allele for dimples and one recessive allele for no dimples (Dd); when their alleles combine during fertilisation, 25% offspring will be DD (dimples), 50% Dd (dimples) and 25% dd (no dimples)

10.4.4

A characteristics, genes, foreign, cells
B 3, 1, 4, 2
C **two** from: organisms can be made resistant to diseases / pests / frost; high-yield plants can be produced; bacteria can be used to produce medicine; other appropriate advantage

D **two** from: concerns that some people may be allergic **or** that long-term consumption could cause health problems; some people feel it is unethical to manipulate an organism's genes; superweeds or pathogens could be created if organisms breed with other species; other appropriate disadvantage

Big Idea 10 Pinchpoint

A this is an incorrect answer – evolution takes place over **many** generations

B this is the correct answer

C this is an incorrect answer – evolution does not **always** take millions of years

D this is an incorrect answer – the organism itself does not change, the characteristic in the **species** changes

Pinchpoint follow-up

A   **a** 0.5% or 1 in 200   **b** 33% or 1 in 3

    c the proportion of the population with the advantageous characteristic increases over time, as the organisms containing this characteristic are more likely to be able to catch prey and so survive and reproduce passing on their advantageous genes; slower organisms are more likely to die without reproducing (or reproducing as many times)

B a few bacteria in the population have resistance to the antibiotic (through a mutation); these survive and reproduce, passing on the gene to the next generation; bacteria without gene are killed; number of resistant bacteria in population increases; after many generations, all bacteria in population have antibiotic resistance

C   **a** pale, camouflaged, dark, eaten, pale, reproduced, soot, dark, camouflaged, decreasing, increasing, dark

    b 47 (occurred quickly as moths have a very short life cycle)

D e.g. 1 – a number of short- and long-necked giraffes; 2 – long-necked giraffes reaching leaves, short-necked giraffes not able to reach; 3 – only long-necked giraffes alive (short-necked giraffes may be drawn dead); 4 – sperm and egg joining together / chromosome with a gene identified; 5 – all long- necked giraffes

Section 3 Revision questions

1   **a**   **i** no individuals of the species are still alive anywhere in the world [1]

      ii climate change / new predator / disease [1]

    b it decreases [1], because biodiversity is a measure of the number of different species in an area [1]

2   **a** protein – to repair body tissues and make new cells; carbohydrates – main source of energy; lipids – to provide a store of energy, insulation and protect organs [2 for all correct, 1 for 1 correct]

    b adds bulk to food [1] to keep it moving through intestine / help waste be pushed out of body / prevent constipation [1]

    c $\frac{2520}{8400} \times 100$ [1] = 30% [1]

    d add Benedict's solution [1], heat (in water bath) [1]; if solution turns orange-red it contains sugar [1]

3   **a**   **i** carbohydrase / amylase [1]

      ii breaks down carbohydrates / starch [1] into glucose / sugar molecules [1]

    b speed up reactions [1] without being used up [1]

    c live on fibre in the intestines [1]; make vitamins / vitamin K [1]

4   **a**   **i** oxygen [1], water [1]   **ii** mitochondria [1]

    b **two** from: anaerobic doesn't need oxygen, aerobic does [1]; anaerobic produces lactic acid, aerobic does not [1]; aerobic transfers more energy per glucose molecule [1]; aerobic produces carbon dioxide and water, anaerobic does not [1]

    c   **i** fermentation (anaerobic respiration in yeast) [1]

      ii microorganism / yeast [1]

5   **a** alveoli / alveolus [1]

    b transfers gas between lungs and blood [1]; CO_2 out **and** O_2 in [1]

    c large surface area [1] and thin wall / wall only one cell thick [1] to maximise rate of diffusion [1]

6   **a** volume = difference between water levels / 4.0 – 0.5 [1] = 3.5 litres [1] [accept correct value for 2 marks without working]

    b **two** from: exhaled air has: lower proportion of oxygen [1]; higher proportion of carbon dioxide [1]; higher proportion of water vapour [1]; is warmer [1] (or converse)

    c e.g., asthma / smoking [1]

7   **a**   **i** natural selection [1]

      ii fossil record [1] which showed changes in a species [1] **or** extinction [1] which showed that different organisms lived in the past [1] **or** named species, e.g. finches [1] which showed changes linked to the species' environment [1]

    b peer review means scientists evaluating each other's work [1], to check for possible errors / mistakes / conclusions not based on evidence [1]

8   **a** nicotine [1]

    b 1 200 000 [1]

    c lung and throat cancer [1]

    d **four** from: smoke contains chemicals that damage the cilia [1], which stops them moving mucus away from the lungs [1]; mucus traps microorganisms [1], so these are held within the lungs / airways [1], which could cause an infection [1]

9   **six** from: organisms in prey species show variation [1]; those most adapted survive **and** reproduce [1]; named adaptation, e.g. fastest [1]; less well-adapted die [1]; genes from most-adapted individuals are passed onto next generation [1]; offspring are likely to display the advantageous characteristic / advantageous characteristic becomes more common [1]; reference to natural selection [1]; process repeated over many generations [1]; over time can lead to the development of a new species [1]

10   **a** a dominant allele will always be expressed if is present [1]; two copies of a recessive allele are needed for it to be expressed in the organism [1]

    b

	Plant 1	
	P	p
Plant 2 P	Pp	pp
p	Pp	pp

[1]

Pp = purple, pp = white; ratio of Pp : pp is 1:1 [1] so 50% white / ½ white, or 1 white : 1 purple [1]

11   **a** take genes from an organism that has a desired characteristic (foreign genes) [1]; place them into a plant or animal at a very early stage of development [1]; as the organism develops it will display the characteristics of the foreign genes [1]

    b **two** from: disease- / pest-resistant plants [1] – higher yields / healthier plants / fewer chemicals used [1]; higher-yield plants [1] – more food produced / less land needed [1]; bacteria that produce medical drugs [1] – treat more people / produced quicker [1]; (other appropriate examples)

12   **six** from: organisms in prey species show variation [1]; those most adapted survive **and** reproduce [1]; named adaptation, e.g. fastest [1]; less well-adapted die [1]; genes from most-adapted individuals are passed onto next generation [1]; offspring are likely to display the advantageous characteristic / advantageous characteristic becomes more common [1]; reference to natural selection [1]; process repeated over many generations [1]; over time can lead to the development of a new species [1]

a   medical drugs treat symptoms / cure disease [1]; recreational drugs have no medical benefit / are taken for enjoyment [1]

b   i   ethanol (alcohol) [1]

   ii   causes liver disease / liver cirrhosis [1], brain damage / stomach ulcers [1], heart disease [1]

c   i   blocks arteries [1]; prevents blood flowing to heart – heart attack / brain – stroke [1]

   ii   320 deaths per 100 000 [1]

   iii   1% or 1.025% [2; allow $\dfrac{1025}{100\,0000} \times 100$ for 1]

13 a   the rabbit offspring inherit half the genetic material from the mother and half from their father [1]

b   i   22 [1]

   ii   44 [1]

14 a   place a leaf in boiling water (to break cell walls / soften leaf) [1]; place leaf in ethanol to remove chlorophyll [1]; place on a white tile and add iodine [1]

b   i   green part of leaf shaded [1]

   ii   photosynthesis can only occur in the green part of the leaf [1] as chlorophyll is needed to absorb light [1]; photosynthesis produces glucose / sugar [1] ; glucose is stored as starch [1]

15 a   found in nucleus [1]; all genetic material is made up of the chemical DNA [1], arranged in long strands called chromosomes [1]; short sections of DNA called genes each code for a single characteristic [1]

b   Franklin and Wilkins [1] took an X-ray of DNA [1], which was then seen by Watson and Crick [1] who worked out DNA is a double helix structure [1]

Periodic table

1	2											3	4	5	6	7	0
7 **Li** lithium 3	9 **Be** beryllium 4											11 **B** boron 5	12 **C** carbon 6	14 **N** nitrogen 7	16 **O** oxygen 8	19 **F** fluorine 9	4 **He** helium 2
23 **Na** sodium 11	24 **Mg** magnesium 12											27 **Al** aluminium 13	28 **Si** silicon 14	31 **P** phosphorus 15	32 **S** sulfur 16	35.5 **Cl** chlorine 17	20 **Ne** neon 10
39 **K** potassium 19	40 **Ca** calcium 20	45 **Sc** scandium 21	48 **Ti** titanium 22	51 **V** vanadium 23	52 **Cr** chromium 24	55 **Mn** manganese 25	56 **Fe** iron 26	59 **Co** cobalt 27	59 **Ni** nickel 28	63.5 **Cu** copper 29	65 **Zn** zinc 30	70 **Ga** gallium 31	73 **Ge** germanium 32	75 **As** arsenic 33	79 **Se** selenium 34	80 **Br** bromine 35	40 **Ar** argon 18
85 **Rb** rubidium 37	88 **Sr** strontium 38	89 **Y** yttrium 39	91 **Zr** zirconium 40	93 **Nb** niobium 41	96 **Mo** molybdenum 42	[98] **Tc** technetium 43	101 **Ru** ruthenium 44	103 **Rh** rhodium 45	106 **Pd** palladium 46	108 **Ag** silver 47	112 **Cd** cadmium 48	115 **In** indium 49	119 **Sn** tin 50	122 **Sb** antimony 51	128 **Te** tellurium 52	127 **I** iodine 53	84 **Kr** krypton 36
133 **Cs** caesium 55	137 **Ba** barium 56	139 **La*** lanthanum 57	178 **Hf** hafnium 72	181 **Ta** tantalum 73	184 **W** tungsten 74	186 **Re** rhenium 75	190 **Os** osmium 76	192 **Ir** iridium 77	195 **Pt** platinum 78	197 **Au** gold 79	201 **Hg** mercury 80	204 **Tl** thallium 81	207 **Pb** lead 82	209 **Bi** bismuth 83	[209] **Po** polonium 84	[210] **At** astatine 85	131 **Xe** xenon 54
[223] **Fr** francium 87	[226] **Ra** radium 88	[227] **Ac*** actinium 89	[261] **Rf** rutherfordium 104	[262] **Db** dubnium 105	[266] **Sg** seaborgium 106	[264] **Bh** bohrium 107	[277] **Hs** hassium 108	[268] **Mt** meitnerium 109	[271] **Ds** darmstadtium 110	[272] **Rg** roentgenium 111	[285] **Cn** copernicium 112	[286] **Nh** nihonium 113	[289] **Fl** flerovium 114	[289] **Mc** moscovium 115	[293] **Lv** livermorium 116	[294] **Ts** tennessine 117	[222] **Rn** radon 86
																	[294] **Og** oganesson 118

*The lanthanides (atomic numbers 58–71) and the actinides (atomic numbers 90–103) have been omitted.

OXFORD
UNIVERSITY PRESS

Great Clarendon Street, Oxford, OX2 6DP, United Kingdom

Oxford University Press is a department of the University of Oxford.
It furthers the University's objective of excellence in research,
scholarship, and education by publishing worldwide. Oxford is a
registered trade mark of Oxford University Press in the UK and in
certain other countries

British Library Cataloguing in Publication Data
Data available

978-1-38-203016-8

10 9 8 7 6 5 4 3

Paper used in the production of this book is a natural, recyclable
product made from wood grown in sustainable forests.
The manufacturing process conforms to the environmental regulations
of the country of origin.

Printed and bound by CPI Group (UK) Ltd, Croydon, CR0 4YY

Acknowledgements

The publisher and authors would like to thank the following for
permission to use photographs and other copyright material:

Cover image: Science Photo Library/Alamy Stock Photo; **p6**: NASA/
Johns Hopkins University APL/Southwest Research Institute; **p15**:
PerWil/Shutterstock; **p18**: parinyatk/Shutterstock; **p29**: Gavran333/
Shutterstock; **p30(L)**: Le Do/Shutterstock; **p30(R)**: Anton-Burakov/
Shutterstock; **p31**: Dario Sabljak/Shutterstock.

All artwork by Aptara Inc., Q2A Media Services Ltd., and Phoenix
Photosetting

Every effort has been made to contact copyright holders of material
reproduced in this book. Any omissions will be rectified in subsequent
printings if notice is given to the publisher.